The Effective Teaching of Modern Languages

THE EFFECTIVE TEACHER SERIES

General editor: Elizabeth Perrott

EDUCATION AND CULTURAL DIVERSITY   by Edward Hulmes

THE EFFECTIVE TEACHING OF ENGLISH   by Robert Protherough, Judith Atkinson and John Fawcett

THE EFFECTIVE TEACHING OF MODERN LANGUAGES   by Colin Wringe

THEORY OF EDUCATION   by Margaret Sutherland

The Effective Teaching of Modern Languages

Colin Wringe

LONGMAN
London and New York

Longman Group UK Limited,
Longman House, Burnt Mill, Harlow,
Essex CM20 2JE, England
and Associated Companies throughout the world.

*Published in the United States of America
by Longman Inc., New York*

First published 1989

British Library Cataloguing in Publication Data
Wringe, C. A. (Colin Alfred), 1937–
  The effective teaching of modern languages. – (The
  effective teacher series).
  1. Schools. Curriculum subjects. Modern Languages.
  Teaching
  I. Title II. Series
  418′.007′1

ISBN 0-582-29719-2

Library of Congress Catalouging in Publication Data
Wringe, Colin.
  The effective teaching of modern languages/Colin
  Wringe.
    p.   cm. – (The effective teacher series)
  Bibliography: p.
  Includes index.
  ISBN 0-582-29719-2
  1. Languages, Modern – Study and teaching. I. Title.
  II. Series.
    PB35.W74 1989   88–21752
    418′.007 – dc19   CIP

Set in Linotron 202 10/11 pt Times

Produced by Longman Group (FE) Limited
Printed in Hong Kong

CONTENTS

Editor's preface   vi

Author's Preface   vii

Acknowledgement   ix

List of Abbreviations   x

1 Defining the task   1

2 Planning   24

3 The receptive skills: listening and reading   42

4 Speaking   56

5 Writing   72

6 Questioning   87

7 Differentiaton in years 1–5   104

8 Language teaching 16–19   120

9 Using aids and technology   134

Bibliography   152

Index   155

EDITOR'S PREFACE

This new series was inspired by my book on the practice of teaching, (*Effective Teaching: a practical guide to improving your teaching*. Longman 1982) written for teacher training students as well as for in-service teachers wishing to improve their teaching skills. The books in this series have been written with the same readership in mind. However, the busy classroom teacher will also find that the books serve their needs as changes in the nature and pattern of education make the retraining of experienced teachers more essential than in the past.

The rationale behind the series is that professional courses for teachers require the coverage of a wide variety of subjects in a relatively short time. So the aim of the series is the production of 'easy to read', practical guides to provide the necessary subject background, supported by references to encourage and guide further reading together with questions and/or exercises devised to assist application and evaluation.

As specialists in their selected fields, the authors have been chosen for their ability to relate their subjects closely to the needs of teachers and to stimulate discussion of contemporary issues in education.

The series covers subjects ranging from *The Theory of Education* to *The Teaching of Mathematics* and from *The Psychology of Learning* to *Health Education*. It will look at aspects of education as diverse as *Education and Cultural Diversity* and *Assessment in Education, The Effective Teaching of English* and *The History of Education*. Although some titles such as *The Administration of Education* are specific to England and Wales, the majority of titles, such as *Comparative Education, The Effective Teaching of Modern Languages, The Use of Computers in Teaching* and *Pupil Welfare and Counselling* will be international in scope.

In a period when education is a subject of general debate and is operating against a background of major change, there is little doubt that the books, although of primary interest to teachers, will also find a wider readership.

Elizabeth Perrott

AUTHOR'S PREFACE

The General Certificate of Secondary Education, and before it
the graded objectives movement, have brought not only a new
set of aims and criteria of achievement in the teaching of modern
foreign languages, but also a whole battery of new teaching techniques. Typically, these include such activities as oral work in
pairs and groups, listening to recorded material for information,
skimming printed ephemera for gist, composing letters, lists and
brief notes, guessing games and many other information gap
exercises. These have become as much a part of the stock-in-
trade of present-day language teachers as were the giving of
dictations and the setting of verb paradigms to be learned to their
predecessors. Between times, whole methodologies of mim–mem
overlearning, audio-visual approaches and background studies
have come, gone and all but passed into oblivion.

Effective teaching in Modern Langauges involves the selection
of appropriate aims and the use of suitable teaching techniques.
Alone, however, these do not suffice, for appropriate aims may
be pursued ineffectually and apparently appropriate methods
ineffectually used. If 'language for communication' is to be more
than a slogan marking our allegiance to whatever is fashionably
modern, its goals must be pursued and its teaching methods
employed with intelligence and understanding, such that a certain
kind of pupil learning is maximised. Criticism, review and self-
evaluation are a constant necessity.

The present handbook attempts, with the hesitancy proper to
a relatively new and unexplored situation, to suggest ways in
which these things might be achieved. Current language teaching
aims and widely accepted approaches to the task of teaching the
various language skills are examined. The specific problems of
teaching at various levels of age and ability are discussed and a
final chapter deals with the management and use of teaching aids
and technology. Each chapter contains proposals for self-review
by either individuals or groups of teachers, and suggestions for
further reading.

Colin Wringe

ACKNOWLEDGMENT

We are grateful to the following for permission to reproduce
copyright material: Thomas Nelson and Sons for an excerpt from
p. 147, *Action! Graded French* by Michael Buckby.

LIST OF ABBREVIATIONS

AEB	Associated Examining Board
A/S	Advanced Supplementary
CALL	Computer Assisted Language Learning
CEE	Certificate of Extended Education
CNAA	Council for National Academic Awards
CSE	Certificate of Secondary Education
DES	Department of Education and Science
FE	further education
GCE	General Certificate of Education
GCSE	General Certificate of Secondary Education
HMI	Her Majesty's Inspectorate
JMB	Joint Matriculation Board
NEA	Northern Examining Association
OHP	overhead projector
SEC	Secondary Examinations Council
SCUE	Standing Conference on University Entrance

CHAPTER 1

Defining the task

In the field of management a distinction is sometimes drawn between efficiency – doing whatever one has decided to do well – and effectiveness, which is a matter of choosing the right thing to do in the first place (Drucker 1967: 1–5). To an extent, the dichotomy is a false one for there is little purpose in choosing appropriate long-term goals if we are muddled and inefficient in our attempts to achieve them. In examining how the tasks of language teaching may most effectively be approached, however, it is well to begin by considering what we should be attempting to achieve before passing to the question of how this is to be done. Unlike some earlier so-called revolutions in language teaching, perhaps, those changes of approach which have most recently taken place provide not only for an array of new classroom techniques but also propose a number of aims which some existing language teachers will find unfamiliar in their emphasis and disturbing in their consequences.

The General Certificate of Secondary Education (GCSE) National Criteria for French, which are explicitly intended to apply to other languages as well, set out seven aims which, with appropriate modification, appear at the head of all modern language syllabuses. These have been arrived at after intensive consultation with teachers themselves as well as with Her Majesty's Inspectorate (HMI), local authority language advisers, teacher educators, language teaching associations and other interested parties. They are:

1. to develop the ability to use French effectively for purposes of practical communication,
2. to form a sound base of the skills, language and attitudes required for further study, work and leisure,
3. to offer insights into the culture and civilisation of French-speaking countries,
4. to develop an awareness of the nature of language and language learning,
5. to provide enjoyment and intellectual stimulation,
6. to encourage positive attitudes to foreign language learning and to speakers of foreign languages and a sympathetic approach to other cultures and civilisations,

7. to promote learning skills of more general application (e.g. analysis, memorising, drawing of inferences).

(DES, 1985: 1)

A number of other desirable aims may be derived both from the National Criteria themselves and from the authoritative HMI publication *Modern Foreign Languages to 16* (DES 1987a: 1–5). These include:

(a) developing a capacity for understanding the unfamiliar by taking pupils out of the familiar environment which is pervaded by English and allowing them to explore the life-style and culture of other lands through the medium of their languages;
(b) promoting social interaction within and beyond the classroom (including interaction with speakers of the foreign language);
(c) improving personal and social skills by learning to communicate, cooperating and contributing in class, considering the views of others and having to adjust to different social conventions.

The recent indication that a foreign language is to be studied by all pupils up to age 16 (DES 1987b: 7) also implies that effective language teaching must engage and be relevant to pupils of all abilities throughout the five years of secondary education. Developments in education generally also suggest that effective teaching approaches in the future will be those that entail active cooperative learning by pupils of a wide range of ability (SEC 1986: 7).

COMMUNICATING IN THE FOREIGN LANGUAGE

That the purpose of learning a modern foreign language is to communicate with those who speak it is no new insight. Other reasons have been given in the past, especially by those who hoped that French and German would come to replace Greek and Latin in the curriculum. But more recently even the most traditional language teachers have regarded communication as their ultimate, if not their immediate, goal. Indeed, the suggestion is sometimes made (Nicholls 1984: 261–9) that so wide and various are the possible interpretations of the term 'communicative' that it may serve as little more than a perfunctory slogan. Yet recent changes in both the aims and the methods of foreign language teaching turn precisely on the distinction between what is and what is not a communicative approach to language teaching.

COMMUNICATIVE AND NON-COMMUNICATIVE APPROACHES

Until very recently it was more or less universally assumed by language teachers that their first priority was to ensure that their pupils should be able to produce and understand the main structures of the language and a consensually agreed range of vocabulary. Teaching methods used – learning vocabulary and paradigms, translating sentences and passages, filling in gaps, questions designed to 'force' the use of certain structures and so on – were all, intended to achieve this purpose. The controversies that raged among modern linguists essentially concerned the question of which methods were more efficient at producing more or less agreed ends. It was supposed that someone who possessed a thorough mastery of the structures of the language and a supply of relevant vocabulary would be able to use it for the purposes of communication, should the need arise.

Certainly some gifted individuals learned to communicate in a foreign language by such means, but few even of the relatively narrow stratum of those with whom language teaching was attempted, ever acquired the ability or confidence to do so.

It is not denied that some of the above methods may sometimes have a valid part to play in language learning. It is a fundamental assumption of a communicative approach, however, that most pupils will best learn to communicate in the foreign language if they spend a good part of their learning time in activities which as closely as possible resemble the act of communicating in a situation they are likely to encounter.

COMMUNICATIVE SYLLABUSES

A first and obvious distinction between communicative and non-communicative approaches to language teaching is to be seen in the way in which syllabuses and courses of study are conceived and set out. In former times, if syllabuses had been spelled out with any precision, which usually they were not, it would have been in terms of structure and lexis, e.g. pupils needed to know the imperfect, but not the subjunctive, the past historic for recognition purposes only, the external and visible parts of the body but not the internal organs (except the heart and lungs), and so on.

The content of textbooks was invariably listed in terms of grammatical structures covered with, perhaps, chapter titles indicating areas of vocabulary and idiom likely to be encountered.

Communicative syllabuses, by contrast, are spelled out in terms of competences, things pupils are supposed to be able to *do* with language.

These so-called language functions have been widely listed as:

1. Giving and seeking factual information.
2. Expressing and finding out about intellectual attitudes.
3. Expressing judgements and evaluations.
4. Getting things done.
5. Socialising.

These broad 'language functions' have been subdivided. For example, 'getting things done' includes among other things:

(a) suggesting a course of action;
(b) offering to do something;
(c) asking others to do something;
(d) asking permission to do something;
(e) saying that something is/is not obligatory;
(f) expressing want or desire, and so on.

(Van Ek 1976: 19–21)

Further specificity may be provided by stating the settings in which those tasks are to be carried out, and in relation to which topics.

Thus, in a restaurant setting, in relation to the topic 'food and drink' it may, for example, be specified that candidates should be able to:

Attract the waiter's attention.
Order a drink or a snack.
Order a meal.
Ask for a particular fixed price menu.
Say how many there are in the group.
Ask for a table for a certain number.
Ask the cost of dishes and drinks . . . etc.

(NEA 1987: 23)

The process of defining language tasks and the settings in which they are to be performed may, indeed, be carried to considerable lengths (Munby 1978: 116–32).

If some language syllabuses also propose minimal lists of structures and vocabulary which candidates need to know in relation to the four language skills of listening, speaking, reading and writing at the basic and higher levels (see NEA 1987: 64–129) the learning of these is not to be regarded as an end in itself but as a means to the end of performing the specified language tasks.

The practice of spelling out objectives in terms of specific things the pupil is supposed to be able to do comes to us not only from developments in general pedagogy (see, e.g. Perrott 1982: 12–15) but also from recent developments in applied linguistics. It has been increasingly realised, especially in the teaching of English as a foreign language but also elsewhere, that the language required for vocational purposes is often fairly specific. Attempts have, in consequence, been made to analyse the particular language requirements of various occupations as well as to define a more general 'threshold level' of competences which all speakers of the language must possess if they are to be functionally viable (see e.g. Jupp and Hodlin 1975; Van Ek 1976: 1–9).

AUTHENTIC TASKS

In a communicative language course the tasks which pupils are taught to perform and the topics and settings to which they relate are characteristically those which might reasonably be expected to confront them in some possible real-life situation. Role-play tasks are typically those in which the English pupil has to deal with a foreign host family, or shopkeeper or official. Reading and listening tasks at an elementary level include public notices and announcements providing information needed by the traveller. Later, more extensive materials for the practice of these skills are those which English teenagers might conceivably read or listen to for interest or information, rather than simply to improve their knowledge of the language. Teachers and course-writers also expend some ingenuity in devising situations in which an English person might need to write lists, messages or letters in the foreign language.

Some Level I graded test syllabuses are specifically defined in terms of situations likely to confront the pupils on a visit to the country with their parents, and higher levels in terms of likely requirements on visits of a more independent kind. We may, however, also imagine authentic situations in which, either now or in the future, pupils may be called upon to deal with a foreign visitor to Britain in the latter's own language.

Among some hard-line reformers of foreign language teaching, 'authenticity', like 'communication' has become something of a slogan word. Some teachers, in consequence have come to feel sheepish or even apologetic about the often highly necessary precommunicative presentation and rehearsal of new language intended for later communicative use, or the employment of materials specially created or edited for teaching purposes. Such feelings are entirely out of place. The only test of valid practice is whether it provides the best means of enabling pupils to communicate successfully or respond appropriately to written and spoken messages in the language in real life. Frequent use of communicative activities and authentic materials in the classroom will certainly be highly conducive to this end. But it is absurd and doctrinaire to rule out other activities and the use of other materials on occasions when these are, in fact, the most economical and effective means available for promoting pupils' learning.

STANDARDS OF ACCEPTABILITY

For many teachers accustomed to marking pupils' work on the basis of 'one mark off per mistake' the most troubling feature of the current approach to foreign language teaching lies in the change of emphasis in the standards of acceptability according to which pupils' efforts are to be appraised. Though GCSE syllabuses continue to allocate marks for accuracy, at least at higher levels, it is stressed that this is to be considered in relation to its ability to facilitate or impede communication (see, e.g. NEA 1987: 130–9). In all cases a proportion of the marks for a given task is set aside for language which would effectively communicate the required message to a sympathetic native speaker however many errors it may contain. The requirements of a communicative approach are no less rigorous than those operating in traditional days when every error was penalised, though they may place greater demands of judgement on those applying them.

Suppose that pupils are asked to write a letter in French to a hotel containing the following points:

1. Say your family would like to book a double room for your parents and a single room for yourself and your grandmother.
2. Ask the price.
3. Say you would like a room on the ground floor for your grandmother if possible.
4. Say you hope to arrive around 8.30 p.m. on the first evening.

In former times candidates would probably have been given less precise instructions regarding the content of their letter, but would have been required to write it in a given number of words. Penalties for missing out part of the message would have been relatively light provided the minimum number of words was achieved. Wrong genders for *prix* and *chambre* would certainly be penalised and the wrong gender for *grand-mère* being a 'gross' error would probably count double.

In a communicative approach, relatively little depends on Granny's gender and a masculine article or possessive would be regarded as a harmless slip of no great significance. The same applies to other minor errors which would not interfere with comprehension, though an accumulation of these might reasonably be thought a distraction which would interfere with the message. Any incoherence, omission or ambiguity likely to lead to one of the four parts of the message not being understood, however, would result in marks for that section being lost, even if the words used were correct French and the grammatical phrases correctly constructed.

In this regard, the penalty might be more severe than in more traditional times when such failure might simply count for 'one mark off' just like any other. It should be added that the sympathetic native recipient of the letter does not have to be a thought-reader, nor does he have to know enough English to be able to guess what the English writer is trying to say. *Des chambres cingles* would therefore cause him some puzzlement and enquiries about *une salle* (as opposed to *une chambre*) *au rez-de-chaussee* might well be misunderstood. Reference to *sales doubles* on whatever floor (a brave attempt in traditional terms) might be expected to strain sympathy to breaking-point.

THE FOUR LANGUAGE SKILLS

A characteristic of the communicative approach as it is currently understood in the English secondary-school context is the equal weighting given to the three language skills of listening, speaking and reading, and also to that of writing in the case of pupils for whom that aim is thought appropriate. It might seem that regarding all four as equally important is somewhat arbitrary, for arguments may certainly be given for regarding some as more important than others. Such arguments, however, are invariably inconclusive and the present situation is certainly more defensible than earlier ones in which productive writing received a major allocation of the marks and reading compehension had to be supplemented by the skill of translating into literary English.

It is an open question whether regarding the four language skills as equally important entails devoting an equal amount of time to teaching them at all stages. In the early weeks one may wish (cf. Page 1986: 9) to control the material introduced fairly closely and work over everything fairly intensively to the point where the class can actually produce it. At later stages the reading of authentic materials for gist and information may come to predominate, at least for some pupils. Until we have more experience on this point it remains appropriate at all stages constantly to review one's teaching to ensure that none of the four skills are being neglected through inadvertence.

Separating the four skills for theoretical or assessment purposes does not mean that we necessarily have to *teach* them separately or avoid the use of multi-skill activities such as carrying on a conversation or responding in the foreign language to spoken or printed material, which are characteristic of everyday communication.

When we are concerned to *test* listening comprehension it may be appropriate to isolate this particular skill by setting multiple-choice questions in English. In this way the interpretation of results is not complicated by the candidates' good or bad performance in other skills. As far as teaching is concerned, however, it may be preferable to use the recording as a basis for oral question-and-answer work in the language. If pupils perform well in this activity it is reasonable to suppose that comprehension is taking place while the oral production skill is being practised as well. Reading, discussing and responding to a letter may be a thoroughly valid teaching strategy even though the performance of pupils will depend on a combination of skills.

COMMUNICATIVE TEACHING METHODS

Like all educational developments, communicative language teaching has produced its own characteristic teaching methods. These naturally include oral work in groups and pairs and the use of flash-cards, cue-cards and other visuals to indicate required responses without recourse to the mother tongue. In information-transfer activities (Abbott and Wingard 1981: 69–77) information given in a non-verbal form is used by the student as a basis for his verbal responses. Such materials may include timetables and information grids, maps, plans and diagrams, symbols with an appropriate key to indicate tourist or other facilities and so on. These provide many opportunities for dialogue work of an imaginative and authentic kind. Information-transfer activities may also be used in both listening and reading comprehension, as when pupils are required to trace a route indicated by travel directions or mark the location of someone's apartment or other meeting-point on a map.

Where possible, not only should utterances and situations be authentic in form but should contain genuine information unknown to the listener. In the fairly recent past the use of the verbs *avoir* and *habiter* and the words for the various family relationships might have been practised with a text about a family living in a certain town. The text would be available to everyone. Questions asked by the teacher, e.g.:

  – Est-ce que les Lebrun habitent a Calais?
  – Non, ils habitent. . . .
  – Combien d'enfants, les Lebrun, ont-ils?

and so on would be meaningful, as would the pupils' replies. Methodologically this would at least be an improvement on simply learning the *habiter* and *avoir* paradigms or translating into French 'The Lebruns live in Bordeaux. They have five children.' Since, however, the answers to these questions are already known to everyone present, they must be regarded as, albeit often very necessary pre-communicative oral practice, rather than true communication.

In a genuinely communicative lesson pupils might practice seeking and giving personal information by conducting a survey of their classmates, asking each other where they live, how many brothers, sisters, pets they have, and so on.

Widely used devices for creating 'information-gap situations' include incomplete grids (pairs of pupils each have, for example, an incomplete timetable and have to fill in the missing information by asking each other), treasure hunts in which one student guides the other to the required spot on a blank plan and numerous other guessing games, card games and competitive activities which depend on the finding or passing of information (see especially Pattison 1987: 35ff).

USING THE TARGET LANGUAGE

Dedicated modern linguists have long insisted that the target language should be used both for incidental classroom business and for teaching purposes. Sometimes the effect of this has been rather comic as when, in the earlier part of this century, adherents of the so-called 'direct method' attempted to use the target language in combination with basically rather traditional approaches. Textbooks of the period often contained such instructions as:

'Apprenez le verbe suivant.'
'Remplacez le tiret par le pronom convenable'.
or
'Traduisez en français!'

Grammatical rules were often explained in language well beyond the comprehension of the pupils for whom it was intended (Wringe 1976: 25–6).

Other amusing foibles still observable in some classrooms include the practice of starting the lesson with some stereotyped pleasantries in the language before reverting to utterly traditional work. The foreign language is also sometimes used to give an instruction which is immediately translated into English and page numbers given orally in the language may also be written on the board. In all such cases use of the language is perfunctory and is ignored by the pupils who know that anything important will be said in English.

Use of the language so often degenerated into mere observance in this way because it bore little relation to the objectives according to which the teacher's performance would be judged. The teacher who asked 'Qui est absent?' or said 'Fermez la fenêtre s'il vous plaît' was simply being virtuous, and virtue must be its own reward.

In a modern communicative approach by contrast, listening comprehension is regarded as a valid achievement, and whether classroom business is successfully carried out provides feedback on whether or not the instructions have been understood. This is genuine communication for which situations do not have to be artificially created, and the time and trouble involved may now make a worthwhile contribution to the achievement of assessable objectives.

Pupils these days are a good deal more mature and ready to cooperate with teachers who treat them sensibly than may have been the case in the 'them and us' atmosphere of many authoritarian classrooms in the past. Certain carefully structured oral approaches to language teaching have also enabled many teachers to acquire skills in presenting usage and meaning without the use of explanation or translation.

These reasons all incline one to take much more seriously the suggestion that teachers should themselves use the target language in the classroom. This does not mean that the mother tongue should never be used. Such blanket prohibitions are a source of anguish to the conscientious and an invitation to self-deception and hypocrisy for others.

A number of important principles of good educational practice also run counter to the ideal of using the target language exclusively. It is desirable that we should relate and interact fairly easily and informally with our pupils. For some, possibly all of them at times, having a satisfactory relationship with adults, including teachers, may be educationally more important than the amount of French or German they learn. It is also regarded as important these days that pupils should fully understand the point of the learning activities they are engaged in and take responsibility for the aims and purposes of their own learning. This entails encouraging pupils to be confident and forthcoming in expressing their own interests, perceptions and understandings of things. This is not likely to take place if speaking the mother tongue is surrounded by a furtive atmosphere of guilt and prohibition.

Certain things more closely connected with the learning of the language – why a certain expression is used, what the speaker intends to be understood but does not actually say and so on – may also best be dealt with in English.

Despite these reservations, however, most teachers who use both the mother tongue and the target language in the classroom could probably tip the balance a bit further towards the latter without great loss. The teacher keen to increase his effectiveness in this regard may therefore find it helpful to monitor his or her use of English, either during the lessons themselves or with the help of sample recordings. Whenever English is used the appropriate response is not 'Oh dear, there I go sinning again' but rather to ask 'Could I in fact have said that in French or German – or achieved the same purpose by saying something simpler?' Or 'Is this an instruction, which I give frequently and which I therefore ought to teach them to recognise in the target language?' If the answer is 'yes', the implications for future action will be obvious. If it is 'no', so be it. One may continue to use English in similar situations with a good conscience. The aim is not exclusive use of the target language but its maximisation, subject to other important considerations.

Once one consciously sets about maximising one's use of the target language, however, it is remarkable how infrequent those occasions on which one *must* revert to English seem to become.

THE NON-LINGUISTIC AIMS

It has been pointed out (DES 1987b: 5) that Aims 2–7 appearing in the GCSE National Criteria do not easily admit to being spelled out in terms of examinable linguistic achievements. Nowadays teachers' work is no longer evaluated solely in terms of examination successes, though they naturally owe it to their pupils to ensure that they gain results which do full justice to their abilities. If modern languages is to merit its place in the curriculum these wider aims must be reflected in the work of modern language teachers. Fortunately, as will become evident in the following pages, the so-called non-linguistic aims are highly compatible with that of developing the ability to use the foreign language effectively for the purposes of communication.

Providing a sound base of skills, language and attitudes required for further study, work and leisure

In the case of many pupils, if the foreign language is used at all it will be in connection with holiday visits to the country where it is spoken. There is therefore nothing inappropriate in the sometimes derided predominance of material concerned with asking the way, booking accommodation, ordering meals, buying motor fuel and so on.

Reference to the requirements of work is more problematic. We do not know what occupations our various pupils will later undertake and probably feel that, except in so far as they impinge on the general public, there is little place in the school language syllabus for parts of the foreign language specifically required by overseas telephone operators, insurance actuaries, international lawyers and tobacco importers. Such learning may be thought part of the strictly vocational training of future employees in those occupations.

In many occupations in which one has to communicate with members of the public, customers, suppliers, visiting colleagues or others outside one's immediate work group, however, certain elementary language skills will sometimes be an advantage. These include the ability to communicate with, comprehend, greet or relate to persons speaking the language of neighbouring countries, as well as reading correspondence, printed instructions and other informative literature. It may be suggested (Emmans, Hawkins and Westoby 1974: 85) that the ability to write a foreign language is less important than the skills of listening, reading and speaking, but it is also likely that the ability to complete simple proformas or provide information or other replies in a comprehensible if not always grammatically perfect form may sometimes be helpful. Occupations to which these comments do not apply become progressively fewer, and to those concerned with communication such as secretarial occupations and jobs in transport, tourism and forwarding, they apply with particular force.

As in the case of leisure use, the desideratum is effective communication, and above all a willingness to communicate at a relatively simple level rather than native-like expression in either speech or writing.

As regards the skills needed for further study, those who are sceptical of recent developments sometimes express disquiet as to whether communicative approaches which attach relatively little importance to grammatical analysis, translation or literary material will provide adequate preparation for advanced level or degree courses. This anxiety rests upon two assumptions which are equally ill-founded.

The first of these is that further courses of language study will forever continue in their present form. Though some such courses may continue to exist, there are signs that they may soon become something of a minority interest among linguists. If recent A-level syllabuses continue to leave some place for translation tests these are clearly intended to be incidental to other modes of acquiring and testing language proficiency. A similar tendency is to be observed in degree and other advanced courses in many of the newer universities and other institutions of higher education. In particular, the place of literary studies in advanced language courses has been under attack for some time (JMB 1984: 3).

The second unjustified assumption is that the most efficient way of achieving even the objectives of more traditional advanced language courses is to begin the grinding study of grammar, the practice of translation and the reading or oral translation of literary or subliterary narrative at an early stage. Grammatical prescriptions encountered before the relevant part of the language is familiar tend to inhibit rather than guide and reinforce.

Even while translating was still used for assessment at 'O' level many successful teachers felt that the most authentic and meaningful translations were produced when the introduction of this skill was delayed until a good deal of language was already known. As for the reading of literary texts, the communicative skill of extensive reading for gist may seem a more relevant preparation than the practice of construing word for word encouraged by older approaches.

We are also becoming increasingly aware that some students may require knowledge of a foreign language for the purposes of specialisms other than languages themselves. Though the foreign language may rarely be an essential medium of instruction, many courses these days offer opportunities for individual study in areas of the student's own choosing and in such cases a fluent reading knowledge of a foreign language may enable a student to undertake an interesting and valuable personal investigation. There are also moves afoot in the Council of Europe (Council of Europe 1987) to encourage cooperative courses between institutions in various countries of the European Economic Community. If our ablest young people are to take advantage of these valuable study opportunities the communicative skills of reading and listening for gist and information and of adapting language for the expression of one's own viewpoint would seem to be of overriding importance.

Reference is made in this second aim to developing not only skills but also attitudes required for work, leisure and further study. Essential among these is the belief that it is normal and rational to deal with foreign speakers in their own language (especially in their own country) and to read foreign printed and written material directly, without requiring an expert translation. Above all the lesson to avoid teaching, but which was taught with such devastating effectiveness in the past, is that the pupil 'was never any good at languages' or that English people, especially English males, are exceptionally incompetent in this respect.

Offering insights into the culture and civilisation of countries in which the language is spoken

Following comprehensive reorganisaton and the political necessity of offering language or language-related studies to pupils of all abilities, courses were developed which contained substantial amounts of background knowledge and were frequently offered under the title of European Studies, French Studies, German Studies, Spanish Studies and so on. Though such courses fulfilled a valuable transitional role they have now been largely superseded by the development of language-teaching approaches accessible to all pupils. It nevertheless remains educationally relevant for pupils to become aware of the possibility of modes of life and experience different from their own, both within and outside their own country.

Understanding another person's experience is part of the essential business of communication and is no doubt the kernel of truth contained in the quip that, so different are the social assumptions of Britons and Americans, that their two countries often seem divided rather than united by a common tongue. It would certainly be possible to speak French, German or Spanish with mechanical perfection yet to constantly be at cross-purposes with native speakers of those languages if we had no understanding of their daily concerns or the way in which life in their countries is organised.

Apart from its instrumental contribution to the processes of communication, however, familiarity with the life of societies other than one's own has long been recognised as an educational aim in its own right, justifying the study of history and literature, as well as ancient and modern languages. Foreign countries are part of the real world in which the child lives and increasingly they impinge on the consciousness of all of us.

The terms 'culture' and 'civilisation' are sometimes felt to be vague and ambiguous. Clearly the so-called 'high culture' is not here primarily being thought of but rather the everyday life of people living in the country and the institutions with which they come into daily contact. No particular items of background knowledge are specified by this aim. The intention is, rather, to encourage a move away from synthetic texts and other materials and promote the use of authentic materials of various kinds. These may include not only printed materials (where possible reproduced in their original format) but also authentic visuals and sound and video recordings which have been subjected to such minimal editing as may be necessary to render them suitable for classroom use.

It is therefore implied by the effective pursuit of this aim that materials will not be chosen or confected for the convenience of demonstrating or practising particular items of language, but also for their ability, directly or indirectly, to impart certain information about the customs and institutions of the country or an aspect of the experience of those who live in it.

Inevitably authentic materials produced for use by native speakers of the language in which they are written will contain innumerable unexplained and taken-for-granted references to the way of life in institutions of the countries where the language is spoken. These will include such things as eating and drinking practices, annual festivals and celebrations, the way shops and services are arranged, courtesies to be observed which differ from those of the pupils' home country and so on. Though it is no doubt important that the amount of time not spent actually prac- tising or experiencing the foreign language should be carefully monitored, such references are to be regarded as opportunities for discussion (of the British as well as the foreign practice) rather than as difficulties to be explained away, passed over or edited out as painlessly as possible. These are not red herrings or inter- ruptions to the language learning process but an important part of the pupil's personal and social education and of the process by which pupils come to appreciate and accept the relativity of institutions, practices and values which many members of the older generation regard as entirely unproblematic. Seen in this light, adequate visuals, sound and video recordings, contacts with schools abroad including pen-friendships, *correspondance sonore* (the exchange of recorded tapes between classes and individuals) and above all educational visits and school-to-school exchanges are not peripheral frills but essential materials and activities without which one of the important aims of the subject cannot be achieved.

Developing awareness of the nature of language and language learning

Many teachers are in some uncertainty as to what is intended by this aim and cynics may think it no more than a respectful genuflexion in the direction of Eric Hawkins and the language awareness lobby (see Hawkins 1984; Donmall 1985).

Despite certain notorious remarks in *English 5–16* (DES 1984: 8–9) the formal description of language in terms of the traditional parts of speech or their more recent equivalents seem in the case of most pupils unlikely to do a great deal to enhance awareness of language, or anything else. A more promising response is to see this aim not as an injunction to graft an additional body of knowledge-content on to the language syllabus, but to teach what one teaches in a liberal and intelligible way so that the pupil is able to come to an understanding of the new language (or new languages) he encounters through his own observation and reflection.

In the absence, however, of any universally accepted notion among language teachers of either the nature of language or how an awareness of that nature is best imparted, the following highly tentative suggestions are made with the intention of provoking reasoned and sensible debate, rather than in any illusion that they express a consensual view with finality.

1. It is an important insight into the nature of language that it does not correspond in any one-to-one way with any underlying or given reality. Different languages divide up and express reality, or rather their speakers' perceptions and interpretations of reality, in different ways. An awareness of this fact is almost forced upon the pupil by his earliest acquaintance with the foreign language. French seems to have three words corresponding to 'the' and two corresponding to 'they' but no distinction is made between his and her. '*Je m'appelle*' seems to correspond to 'my name is', but there is no word for name. The French seem to talk about a hat yellow instead of a yellow hat but no one falls about laughing. The German words for 'you' and 'they' sound the same but surprisingly this does not appear to give rise to confusion. Germans also seem to see nothing wrong in writing *Mann* or *Haus* with capital letters even in the middle of a sentence.

Intelligent and lively pupils are bound to remark on these facts. It is submitted that such observations should not be brushed aside as time-wasting or likely to give rise to embarrassing 'Why'? questions which cannot be answered, but encouraged: 'Yes, and you will find there are lots of other differences too, as we learn more.' Where such discussion does not arise spontaneously, it may be provoked. 'Anyone notice any differences . . .?'

2. Language, as we saw earlier, is not simply for making true statements about the world, but for doing things, and especially for influencing the actions, perceptions and feelings of others. Often the same general message can be communicated in a number of ways. The speaker or writer has considerable freedom in the mode, style or register he employs, depending on just how he wants the other person to feel or react. The whole message is not always contained in the literal meaning of what is said.

This insight is fundamental to such disciplines as literary interpretation, rhetoric and effective speaking and writing, as well as to one's general social competence. It is also essential if pupils are really to understand the workings of either their own language or that of other countries or truly possess them for their own purposes.

Presented in the right way the point is not beyond the understanding of even relatively slow children. One can simply set one's class to make up and practise dialogues with an imaginary exchange partner to practise the 'giving and seeking of personal information'. This is entirely acceptable, but the task can be presented in a slightly different light:

You want to get to know this person don't you? Otherwise you're going to have a miserable time mooching about by yourself. Better ask her a bit about herself – show an interest. No, of course she won't think you're a Nosey Parker. She doesn't want to spend the evening by herself either, does she? Anyway, say a bit about yourself as well, so she doesn't feel as if she is being cross-examined.

At a slightly higher level it might be worth eliciting from a class that when the lady in the shop says (Peck and Jury 1987: recording) 'Wir haben diesen neuen Pullover in warmen Farben. Schön für den Winter, nicht?' she is not simply describing her wares, but selling them. Likewise, when the customer replies, 'Ja, schön sind sie, auch sehr preiswert aber für mich ein bißchen zu klein', the first part of the sentence is not included simply to practise inversion or use of the adjective *preiswert*, but because the speaker is a considerate lady who does not wish to hurt the helpful assistant's feelings or appear rude or abrupt.

In order to give due recognition to this aim, teachers do not need specifically to state these points at any length, but simply be sensitive to occasions on which they can economically be made. Part of one's planning and preparation will involve briefly scanning one's material for such opportunities, or creating them from time to time if necessary.

Providing enjoyment and stimulation

There is no magic formula for ensuring that one's lessons are enjoyable and stimulating. The first requirement is vigilance and self-monitoring. The class that shows unmistakable signs of boredom and understimulation (Perrott 1982: 93–101) may actually *be* bored and understimulated. The reason may lie in one's preparation, or lack of it for if time is not taken to rethink one's teaching, one slips all too easily into doing more of what one did yesterday, or has been doing, without incident or difficulty, for many years.

General injunctions to 'introduce more variety into one's lessons' are unhelpful. One may need to do more than simply spice up one's lessons with jokes, competitions and other forms of extrinsic motivation. Obvious attempts to please or entertain one's class are patronising and often resented. A more profitable approach is likely to be a review of:

1. The nature and level of the tasks being demanded of pupils.
2. The content of the materials being used.
3. One's manner and approach.

Pupils may be alienated either because what is required of them is so difficult that they never have the satisfaction of mastery and achievement, or because it is so banal and unde-manding that it presents no challenge and furnishes no cause for pride even when performed perfectly. One can never be quite sure how a class will respond to a particular task and needs to be sensitive to feedback and ready to review the assumptions underlying one's scheme of work.

Contentwise many older-style courses contained little of intrinsic interest to normal inquisitive teenagers, and were simply concocted to exemplify or practise certain structures or areas of vocabulary. Characters were usually 'nice' children, or in the case of adults, highly respectable fathers and mothers, worthy shop-keepers or middle-aged gentlemen working in offices. Though such characters may be passionately interesting to schoolteachers they scarcely make compulsive reading or viewing for most pupils of secondary-school age.

Language teachers should not perhaps entirely embrace the values of pop culture, but authentic materials intended to be read by teenagers with interest and pleasure are likely to be more interesting *and* intellectually more stimulating than many past offerings. Information about the lives of actual French, German or Spanish children of their own age, recorded by them or accompanied by photographs, are of more obvious interest than the doings of an anaemic Marcel and Denise, not to mention l'Oncle Jules and his talking monkey.

Children at school are, of course, interested in the concerns and problems of adults, but of attractive *young* adults rather than those of their parents' generation. It is sometimes supposed that if a teacher does not already have a stimulating or engaging personality there is nothing that can be done about it. This is by no means entirely true. The cultivation of a bright, impactful manner is largely a matter of effort. The way one enters the class-room, insists on attention (without being neurotic about absolute silence) and above all engages individuals, are matters of self-management rather than innate characteristics. Children like to be noticed as individuals but not embarrassed by excessive atten-tion. Knowledge and use of their names, an interest in their individual personalities, and some acquaintance with their inter-ests and activities out of school are bound to make the experience of working together a more profitable and agreeable one for all concerned.

Happily the achievement of this aim is made easier by the use of such characteristically communicative activities as pair work, group work and information-gap work of various kinds. These provide ample opportunity for pupils to interact with each other – something they naturally find more enjoyable than traditional teacher-centred lessons in which the majority of the class looks passively on while the teacher interacts with one or two individuals, or conducts a monologue.

Encouraging positive attitudes to foreign language learning and to the speakers of foreign languages, and a sympathetic approach to other cultures and civilisations

In an important way, the teacher whose pupils gain high grades in their examination but say 'Thank God, I shall never have to study French or German again' has failed. Ideally one would hope that many pupils who go on to pursue further studies or occupations essentially unconnected with foreign languages will at least maintain their interest, even if they do not actually have occasion to extend their skills. Above all, one hopes they will commend and encourage language study by others, including their own children in due course.

The task of encouraging positive attitudes to language learning will depend in large measure on successful achievement of the previous aim of providing intellectual stimulation and enjoyment, as well as a course which leaves pupils feeling that they have actually acquired the ability to communicate with foreign speakers and other skills relevant to further study, leisure and work.

Materials which authentically acquaint pupils with the lives of their contemporaries in Germany, France, Spain or wherever are likely to be helpful in combatting uncomplimentary stereotypes, as are visits and correspondence bringing pupils into actual contact with speakers of those countries' languages. Familiarity does not necessarily lead to uncritical acceptance, nor indeed should this be looked for (DES 1987(a): 2). The tensions associated with exchange visits may also lead to temporary outbursts of hostility. Teachers accompanying school parties returning home after a successful exchange will often have been appalled by the way in which otherwise well-behaved and receptive pupils 'let off steam' about French table manners or German food. These are no doubt matters for frank and open discussion at a suitable time, as is any tendency to respond negatively or dismissively to cultural or other differences. Discussion of the attitude we should take to differences between ourselves and others is naturally not limited in application to differences between ourselves and particular continental countries. It applies equally to differences with more distant parts of the world and alien political regimes, as well as differences with unfamiliar social and cultural groups in our own country.

The aim must be, firstly, to encourage the welcoming of unfamiliarity and accurate information and, secondly, the forming of balanced judgements on the basis of knowledge rather than prejudice or hostility.

PROMOTING LEARNING SKILLS OF MORE GENERAL APPLICATION

The National Criteria suggest as examples of these more general skills: analysis, memorising and the drawing of inferences. Many language teachers will baulk at all three of these suggestions for in the past these terms, narrowly interpreted, have been associated with unprogressive teaching approaches. Hopefully, however, analysis is not here intended to be synonymous with formal grammatical analysis and memorisation is not to be taken as the rote learning of word lists or paradigms.

The performance of any language task such as becoming acquainted with someone, making a purchase, or writing a letter of enquiry, proceeds according to a certain recognisable pattern. Recognition of this pattern will be helpful to the pupil in performing the task, and is the result of analysis, as is the recognition of analogies, which is the most efficient of all language-learning skills. These examples must serve to stand for the many ways in which effective language teaching both depends on and develops the skill of analysis. Teachers will make their own decisions as to whether the steps they take to develop this skill will be covert or explicit.

Memorisation is more problematical, both in terms of its educational value and as a skill that can be improved by practice. There is also some doubt as to how much use language teachers would want to make of memorisation as a teaching method (but see Buckby *et al*. 1986: 45). Our aim as language teachers should not be that certain words, phrases, dialogues or whatever should be learned off and stored for future recall, as if the brain were a kind of built-in reference book, but that they should become part of the child's linguistic behaviour in appropriate situations. Practice and experience are certainly necessary to this, but are rather different from what is normally thought of as memorisation. If, however, the term is broadly interpreted to mean the careful study and an attempt to fully understand and rehearse what is to be learned, then no doubt this can be seen as both a useful language-learning technique and a habit of more general application.

The drawing of inferences is perhaps more apposite here. Certainly it is an ingredient of general intelligence enabling the individual to acquire knowledge which, in Bruner's phrase, (Bruner 1972: 93) goes beyond the information given. The development of this ability is part of the skill of aural and especially reading comprehension.

A competence in this skill is achieved not by knowing the literal meaning of every word in advance but by developing the habit of considering what the speaker or writer *must* mean given the context and whatever clues are provided by the words themselves. When the writer's or speaker's intention is not literally contained in the actual words given, effective teaching will entail drawing attention to this fact. The habit of interpreting, as opposed to simply decoding, what is said does not come naturally to all children and may need to be taught.

In addition to analysis, memorisation and the drawing of inferences, other learning skills of general application to be acquired in the course of language learning may include the appropriate use of reference works and source materials, both printed and in audio-visual form, the drafting, polishing and orderly presentation of written work, note-taking and revision, rehearsal and discussion with fellow students, listening and reading for information, active participation and discussion and, perhaps above all, a willingness to risk making mistakes as a means of acquiring knowledge.

REVIEW AND ENHANCEMENT

The purpose of this section in this and following chapters is to provide readers with a specific opportunity to incorporate suggestions arising from the text into their own classroom practice. For the most part this is done by inviting them to review their current performance in the light of a number of questions and, if it seems desirable, to modify their future planning and classroom activity accordingly.

It will normally be suggested that the process of review be carried out on the basis of personal recollection supported by reference to teaching notes or, where possible, recordings. It will then be proposed that a series of future lessons be planned and once again be reviewed and, where appropriate, modified in the light of considerations arising from the earlier review of previous work.

Some such methodical process seems desirable if this book is to have its maximum value in contributing to the effectiveness of classroom practice. If it can be carried out in cooperation with a colleague or fellow students, so much the better. Hopefully the book may also sometimes serve as a basis for group work in initial or school-based in-service training.

Activities

1. Reconstruct in detail your work with a particular class during the previous fortnight. As far as possible, list the actual activities undertaken by the pupils.
   (a) Attempt to specify what you intended pupils to learn as a result of each activity.
   (b) Select five activities at random. Consider in each case whether the objective was 'communicative' (were pupils learning to say, write or understand something they might need to say, write or understand in a real situation?), or whether it would be best described as 'knowledge of the language', i.e. of its structure and vocabulary.
   (c) If the latter, was this precommunicative knowledge later put to use in a genuinely communicative activity?
   (d) Plan a further two or three lessons in detail. Subject your proposed activities to review as above. Identify non-communicative activities. Consider whether the objectives of these can be achieved by more authentically communicative tasks, or contribute to other communicative activities directly. If not, consider whether they should be omitted.
2. With the aid of a recording consider each use of English by you in a particular lesson.
   (a) Analyse the purpose or purposes served by the utterance and consider whether it could have been achieved by use of the foreign language, possibly in a simpler form.
   (b) If English was used for explanation, consider whether explanation was necessary at all or whether it could have been replaced by an instruction or question in the foreign language, or simply demonstrated by an example.
   (c) Attempt to quantify your use of English by counting instances or logging time. Repeat the process periodically with a view to achieving a progressive reduction.
3. Prepare schemes of work for two to three weeks, using Aims 2–7 (see p. 1–21) as a checklist. Identify the activities which will enable contributions to be made to the advancement of each of these.
   (a) Select about five further activities at random. Consider how each of these might be modified or presented to enhance their contribution to one or more of the non-linguistic aims without substantially increasing the time required.
   (b) Identify any of the non-linguistic aims to the achievement of which no contribution is made by the schemes. Consider how a number of existing activities could be modified to remedy this or, if necessary, introduce some additional activities for this purpose.

FURTHER READING

Buckby M *et al* 1987
Teaching Modern Languages for the GCSE. British Association for
Language Teaching/Modern Languages Association, Leeds
DES 1985
*General Certificate of Secondary Education; National Criteria for
French*. DES, London
DES 1987
Modern Foreign Languages to 16. HMSO, London
Pattison P 1987
Developing Communication Skills. Cambridge University Press,
Cambridge
Van Ek J A 1975
The Threshold Level. Council of Europe, Strasburg pp. 1–35

The GCSE language syllabuses of various examining groups, notably
those of the Northern Examining Association (NEA), also repay careful
reading.

CHAPTER 2

Planning

THE NEED FOR PLANNING

One of the most striking changes in the lives of teachers during recent years has been the greatly increased amount of time they are now obliged to spend in administration and planning, both in relation to the running of the school as a whole and to their actual work in the classroom. This is nowhere more evident than in the case of modern language teachers.

Partly, this is because of the changed nature of our classes and the changed conditions under which we work. Principally, however, it results from our current conception of language teaching and its aims and the new teaching methods, materials and courses these have brought into being.

The materials for a particular language lesson are nowadays rarely contained between the covers of a single book brought to the lesson by the pupils themselves on pain of lines or detention. Responsibility for ensuring that recorders, cassettes, film-strips, projector and screen, flash-cards, work-sheets, photocopies and regrettably often also the main course-book itself are to hand necessarily falls upon the teacher. When resources must be shared with colleagues this entails arrangements for coordination, however informal, and possibly even advance-booking procedures for equipment and materials.

There is also considerable need for coordination regarding what is learnt when. Current examination syllabuses require pupils to be able to do such specific things as giving directions in a town, asking the times of trains, writing letters, making particular kinds of enquiry, apologising for misunderstandings or accidents and so on. To have covered all the main structures and met a fair range of vocabulary, followed by two or three terms of 'examination practice' is no longer sufficient.

Departmental schemes of work, which may themselves have to be produced in a joint planning exercise, are necessarily detailed and individual teachers are responsible for ensuring that their group remains in contact with the progress of others at the same stage.

Within a particular lesson or series of lessons the timing and sequencing of activities also require planning. Learning to perform particular linguistic functions in specific situations may entail setting up an activity which needs to be carried through to completion within the compass of a single lesson. Unlike traditional grammar exercises consisting of disconnected sentences, these cannot be started at whatever random point in time the class gets to them and broken off when the bell goes. Pupils who do not quite succeed in mastering the appropriate phrases when the lesson comes to an end risk having wasted the whole lesson, while the five minutes required to finish off this lesson's activity cannot be satisfactorily tacked on at the beginning of the next. Even the receptive skills of listening and reading cannot satisfactorily be undertaken on a line-by-line basis, but need to be approached as wholes if the exercise is to resemble an authentic task of reading or listening for gist or information.

In the modern comprehensive school, forms, streams and sets are also somewhat less stable units than they were in the past. They may be re-formed or reorganised as a result of changes in policy or staffing or as a result of larger demographic changes outside the school. The regular teacher is more often absent from the classroom than his predecessor as a result of meetings, in-service training, school trips and other requirements placed upon him. Consequently there is a need specifically to plan the class's work ahead, taking due cognisance of what is being done elsewhere, and to maintain adequate class records, rather than rely on inspiration and personal continuity.

Happily, the requirement to spend additional time in planning is to some extent offset by a reduction in the need for line-by-line preparation, not to mention the nightly chore of detailed marking which many language teachers felt obliged to undertake when writing was regarded as pre-eminent among the language skills, and performance was assessed on a basis of one mark off per mistake.

GAINING A GENERAL OVERVIEW

Little can be said here about planning at managerial level. No doubt, effective teaching depends in large measure upon appropriate staffing, staff deployment and development, resourcing, the disposition of rooms, equipment and so on. Our present concern, however, is with the task of planning to be undertaken by the individual classroom teacher.

Effective performance of this task entails at least some thinking at a general level, as well as a long-term overview of the five-year course and its objectives as a whole. Only thus is it possible to see present work in its due perspective and appropriately adjust the emphasis of one's work in the light of what has gone before and what is to follow. An initial overview of the forthcoming year's work is also particularly helpful. From this it may become apparent that some units are more interesting and have more potential than others. Some may be more difficult or contain more material and so need extra time or are best not begun near the end of term. Equally, one may become aware in good time of units that seem thin and may need supplementing and one may therefore be on the lookout for suitable additional materials or ideas for exploitation. By knowing in advance roughly what one will be doing at some future time one enables one's imagination and subconscious to work on it in one's off-duty hours, before the problem becomes pressing.

One becomes aware that certain pieces of language, certain skills, classroom activities and procedures will occur again and again throughout the year. They are therefore worth spending extra time and trouble on first time round to ensure that they are efficiently mastered from the start. Other, rather complicated activities or unduly time-consuming pieces of material may be isolated or marginal, and may therefore be either omitted or dealt with fairly perfunctorily. It may be apparent that certain visual aids, flash-cards, diagrams or transparencies may come in more than once and are worth making with some care in a fairly permanent form. Some flash-cards provided by the course may be useful, but need supplementing with one or two extra examples, and so on.

One's general overview may enable one to formulate general assumptions about the kinds of activity that arise naturally out of the materials provided or, on the contrary, are not likely to be successful in the light of the class's age, supposed ability, or other things known about them. Such reflections on the kinds of activities likely to constitute the ingredients of one's lessons will naturally entail a consideration of the rooms, facilities and lesson times available.

Group work involving a good deal of movement and dramatic performances may work splendidly in a carpeted studio on Tuesday morning, but not be such a good idea on Friday afternoon in a crowded room with heavy old-fashioned desks and Marley floor tiles. The language laboratory or a language room with a screen, projector facilities and earphone sockets may be available once a week and if one wants to make use of these things one needs to arrange one's weekly pattern of activities accordingly. If, once a week, one is timetabled in a rather distant part of the school that had better not be the day on which one normally starts a new unit, for that will probably be the occasion on which most visuals and other equipment are likely to be required. If double periods are timetabled they may be seen either as a problem to be overcome (How does one occupy a lowest-stream third form with a notoriously short attention span for 80 minutes?) or as an opportunity to do a sustained and integrated sequence of activities on a particular topic. Either way it is better to have devised some general strategy for using the time than to be faced with a crisis of inspiration or a sense of missed opportunity every week.

The overview also involves a consideration of the overall balance of activities. Does the course provide adequate reading or listening materials? Are the proposed writing tasks adequately demanding, or sufficiently simple for this group? How much time and effort ought to be specifically set aside for role-play and other oral production exercises? At what point in each unit are they most conveniently undertaken? What form will homework normally take? On what nights will it be done, and in consequence which lessons each week need to be planned to allow time for it to be adequately explained and prepared for? How often will it be taken in to be marked and how often gone over or seen in class? In considering this final question teachers will necessarily have regard to their own loading and the distribution of their commitments both in the weekly cycle and over the year.

This process can, of course, only be undertaken in very general terms in advance of meeting one's class and beginning work with them. One's projected pattern of work must necessarily remain tentative and subject to change from week to week. Provided it is not too rigid, however, a predictable pattern of work is not disagreeable to most pupils, and may be a source of pleasant anticipation. From the teacher's point of view it has the great advantage of providing a sense of security and removing the need to begin the planning of each individual lesson *de novo* in the course of a busy term. Though this does not avoid the need to plan both individual lessons and longer units of work with care, it may reduce the degree of effort and stress involved, as well as making it easier to maintain an even pace of work in the face of fluctuating pressures from other directions.

UNIT PLANNING

Few things are as inefficient and time consuming as 'one-off' lesson planning at short notice. Such an approach to the planning task risks turning every evening into an anxious search for inspiration and every morning before registration into a frantic dismantling and disentangling of cassettes, film-strips and apparatus that have been unvisited and unloved during the last 12 months. At the very least one needs to think in terms of unit-sized periods of some two to three weeks or more, depending on the course being used.

In the planning of such a unit of work it is valuable strategy to begin by identifying some terminal or culminating activity. This may be the performance of an extended role-play, the writing of a fairly challenging letter either together in class or for homework, reading or listening to a fairly difficult or extended piece of material for detailed information. Once this has been identified, planning consists of working backwards as it were through various learning activities which will enable it to be successfully achieved. These will naturally be suggested by the materials available in the course-book and elsewhere, but their order and selection will not be determined by the order in which they appear in either the pupils' book or the teacher's manual.

The culminating activity of the unit naturally needs to embody the teacher's main objectives for the unit spelled out, as stressed in the previous chapter, in terms of what pupils are expected to be able actually to do in the language. These may well not be the objectives identified by the course-book, for it is the responsibility of the teacher, not the course-book writer to ensure that the learning activities of his class are in line with the requirements of his syllabus. The teacher will also wish to make his own professional judgement as to how far various objectives may realistically be achieved by his particular group.

Activities leading up to the culmination of a unit need to be reviewed to ensure that certain criteria are being met. Important among these is the balance between the four language skills. A unit of work may be intended to culminate in a piece of extended role-play which is, in itself, an achievement in the field of oral production. But the language necessary for this performance may well first be met in the course of listening or reading, and may be consolidated by means of a writing task.

It is not necessary to spend exactly the same amount of time on each of the four skills in every unit. Some situations lend themselves to one kind of work rather than another. Many valuable activities, such as conversation or the discussion of a text or recording involve the use of several skills simultaneously and it is, in any case, fallacious (Wringe 1976: 34) to suppose that language met in the practice of one skill will not enhance one's performance in another. One needs, however, to identify any systematic imbalances in the course as a whole or such obvious deficiences in a particular unit as may easily be corrected. It is also desirable to review the plan of one's unit with regard to the achievement of the various non-linguistic aims considered in Chapter 1.

Human nature being what it is, it is essential to set at least a provisional date for one's culminating activity. If one does not, there is a danger that work on the topic will dribble on in a series of not very productive activities and pieces of work simply because other pressures prevent one from getting round to the task of planning the next unit. One naturally needs to allow ample time for pupils to learn from and enjoy their various activities, but it is better to have to select from among the most beneficial of those one has planned than to continue in order to wring the last drop of learning from a given topic.

Not the least advantage of planning work on a unit in this integrated way is that it provides the teacher with a sense of purpose and achievement that a set of disconnected lessons which just happen to be on the same topic do not. Pupils also gain a sense of progression as the linguistic material becomes increasingly familiar and the various elements build on to each other allowing them to do and say more and more complex things. The clean and predictable break and move on to a new topic after a final demanding and successful performance also have considerable motivational value.

Planning by longish units before coming down to the actual business of lesson planning also has the advantage of separating the question of *what* is to be done from that of *when* it is to be done. If one has given some thought to the overall planning of a unit of work, the planning of individual lessons is largely reduced to arranging one's various activities in the most advantageous order in given blocks of 40 minutes.

PLANNING INDIVIDUAL LESSONS

Defining one's objectives

As with all creative thinking, lesson planning may not always begin with objectives, as logic would have us believe, but with an activity or piece of material which happens to be available, or comes to one's attention. Once one has identified the activity or material, however, it is essential to then define carefully the objectives one will seek to achieve by its means. Without some such clarification one is unable to decide promptly in the classroom which things need to be stressed, insisted upon and thoroughly checked and which can be passed over more lightly in the realisation that they may be picked up by some pupils and, perhaps, missed by others.

One may decide, for example, that a picture of a baker's shop and its contents, together with a short recorded dialogue between the baker and his customer will provide a useful basis for work leading up to an extended shopping role-play. Leaving aside for a moment the question of timing, the following sequence of activities may suggest itself:

1. Question and answer work on the picture to establish vocabulary for the various common forms of French bread (*une baguette, une ficelle, un grand pain, une brioche, des croissants*).
2. Class listening to the dialogue and identifying what is being asked for, and the price of each item.
3. Elementary pair work. A price list is provided. After brief rehearsal pupils take it in turns to ask for various quantities of *baguettes, croissants*, etc. while the baker calculates the price.
4. More complicated pair work for some pupils. The baker, deletes two of the five items without showing his partner, so that question 'Avez-vous . . .?' can be answered by 'Oui, j'ai/Non, je n'ai pas de . . .' and the dialogue continued accordingly.
5. Pupils writing down the baker's price list, a shopping list or a note asking a friend to go and buy so many *croissants, baguettes*, or whatever.

No doubt many pupils would learn quite a lot in the course of these activities even if no great care were taken to identify the main objectives. A little thought, however, might make it clear that:

1. Though some of these activities may involve a good deal of shopping language which has been met before and will certainly be met again, the terms for the various kinds of bread are essential new vocabulary which may not be met so frequently, and needs to be firmly established.
2. This is an exceptionally good opportunity to establish the cultural point that bread comes in a number of different and intriguing forms in France and that, in general, any number of taken-for-granted, everyday things may be done in different ways in different places.

We shall therefore ensure that the names of all five kinds of bread are used over and over again and can be produced by the *weakest* members of the class. To be on the safe side we shall also make a point of asking one of our less alert pupils what he thinks a *baguette* is made of, or what he would ask for if he had some nice French cheese and wanted something to eat with it. Possibly we might also ask what other differences they know between English and French food and drink.

These are our principal objectives, one linguistic, one arising out of two of the non-linguistic aims (Aims 2 and 5) mentioned in Chapter 1. We are particularly concerned that they should be established for all pupils, for such a convenient opportunity is unlikely to occur again. If other things are learned as well, so much the better, but they will not be pressed with such insistence or quite so thoroughly checked.

Identifying one's presuppositions

A common reason why things go wrong in language lessons is that though the new material whose use forms the ostensible objective of the lesson has been carefully presented, some of the language required by the activities designed to practise it has not been met or has been forgotten.

Lessons involving prices or the calculation of bills will be inhibited if pupils are not first fully fluent with numerals, at least over the required range. Enquiries about trains and arranging to meet people go better if telling the time has been given a bit of practice first and practice in apologising will be less constricted if the class has had some experience of 'saying what they have done' (i.e. using past tenses) in other contexts. In designing one's activities, therefore, one needs to ask what else (apart from the new language being taught) do pupils need to know for this activity to be successful? Sometimes a quick formal revision will suffice. On other occasions the required language may need to be taught separately first.

Materials and props

If one does not actually list these when planning one's lesson, individual items may easily be forgotten in the heat of a busy day. Even when teaching in one's own room it is useful to bring various props together quickly before the start of an activity, rather than interrupt proceedings to look for them in drawers or behind cupboards, or to plug in or load recorders. Needless to say, it is also desirable to check the availability and correct functioning of apparatus well before the imminent arrival of the class for whom it is intended.

Attractive and authentic visuals both stimulate interest and provide cultural background. Some teachers devote considerable time, energy and artistic talent to the creation of posters, flashcards, transparencies and so on, and this is something one would hesitate to discourage. It is important, however, to preserve a due proportion between the effort that goes into creating and transporting impressive aids and materials and the actual pay-off in terms of pupils' learning. It is obviously wise to familiarise oneself with aids and materials in the school as well as those on the market with a view to recommending purchase when the opportunity arises. The sensible aim should be to supplement rather than duplicate these – for there is no justification for teachers' time being spent painfully producing materials that can reasonably be purchased. Teachers' own aids need to be simple, comprehensible, attractive and above all stoutly produced for it is obviously an inefficient use of time to produce, inadequately and hurriedly, virtually the same aid year after year.

Timing and the order of activities

Even when one is following a course-book or other prearranged set of activities it will often be necessary to select from among them or rearrange the order in which they are to be undertaken. This is not only for reasons of variety and motivation but in order to avoid substantial or important activities being interrupted at the end of the lesson.

Though it is important to make clear estimates of the time required by various activities, however, these need to be flexible. There is no point in hurrying on when an activity is proving profitable, or allowing it to drag on once pupils have drawn all possible benefit from it. One also needs a clear idea of which activities may be abbreviated or dispensed with should the need arise, and which one would wish to preserve at all costs.

Let us consider the sequence of baker's shop activities referred to in an earlier section, supposing that we are teaching a reasonably well-motivated group of second-formers of no exceptional ability. Our first provisional list of activities and timings might look roughly as follows:

1. Discussion of picture	15 minutes
2. Presentation of recorded dialogue	7 minutes
3. Pair work 1: shopping dialogue	7 minutes
4. Pair work 2: J'ai/je n'ai pas	7 minutes
5. Informal testing and remediation	7 minutes
6. Writing	7 minutes
7. Checking and correcting written work	3 minutes

References to three or seven minutes may seem somewhat clinical and precise. In lesson planning, however, it is well to remember that though some very necessary tasks may take well under five minutes, it is a cardinal error to allow no time for them at all. In a tight schedule the two or three unbudgeted minutes may make the difference between bringing one's lesson to a satisfactory conclusion and an unsatisfactory culminating activity carried through too hastily or cut short by the bell. Many typical classroom activities, on the other hand, seem to require slightly more than five minutes, whereas to allow ten minutes for pairwork activity, for example, may leave the lesson rather slack.

On the estimated timings given the above list of activities would occupy almost an hour, so that if even in a 45-minute period we were to flat-footedly stand up and teach until we hear the bell the final writing activity, at least, would be lost. We might feel that this did not greatly matter, or that this activity could most easily be left over till the next lesson, but we should prefer to make this decision for ourselves in advance rather than have it made for us by the end of the lesson

In planning for a 45-minute period we should, in fact, be looking for activities to occupy not much more than 40 minutes for we must release our class promptly, but cannot be certain they they will arrive on time. If our lesson is too tightly scheduled, opportunities to relate to our pupils and develop and expand their own experiences will be brushed aside. Interested queries and genuine attempts to contribute may be put down as 'interruptions' in the attempt to complete a preordained plan.

Let us add some further details to our picture.

1. In the course of our lesson we have to spend some time returning and commenting on previous written work. Ideally this would take between five and ten minutes.
2. On the other hand, there is a homework slot available this evening.
3. We are not guilty of the traditionalist error of attaching exclusive importance to written work. Though there are few high-flyers in this class, however, we think that, as a group at this stage they will benefit from being given the encouragement and opportunity to do good, careful, neatly presented written work. This includes those members of the class, as yet unidentified, for whom writing may not ultimately be a course objective. This need is made the more pressing as the class does not have a course-book to keep, so that their exercise books are their main means of consolidation and revision.

Clearly we must amend and rearrange our list of proposed activities, for otherwise we shall not have time to test whether our main objectives have been achieved and be at a loss for a sensible homework to set.

One possible adjustment might seem to be to slim down the opening, teacher-centred work on the picture. Though this activity is not, in itself, communicative, however, it is necessary precommunicative preparation for what is to follow. It would be a mistake to cut back on this phase of the lesson too much, for if our key vocabulary items are not firmly in place by the time we leave it, practice in the skills of listening comprehension, oral production in the pair-work activities and the writing exercise will be less confident than they need be.

This is also likely to be the part of the lesson in which a number of non-linguistic aims are met. Pupils may wish to remark that not only does bread in France not come in the same sizes and shapes as in Britain, but the French do not seem to use a general word for a loaf of bread as we do. Neither words, nor things, nor the relationship between them seem to correspond in any one-to-one sort of way (Aim 3).

Nevertheless, in order to take account of uncertainties about the starting time of the lesson one might resolve to complete this activity within say 15 minutes of the official time it is scheduled to begin, leaving some 25 minutes for the remainder of what one hoped to do.

Moving to the other end of the lesson, it is helpful to consider what is necessary if we are to make good use of the available homework period. This might be to write one's note asking someone to buy certain things at the bakery, one's list of what one has spent one's 10 francs on, one's price list to enable one to help the baker by serving in his *boulangerie* and so on, plus perhaps drawing the things to be bought in the baker's shop and writing the names underneath.

That would be a wholly reasonable half-hour's homework and practise important writing and presentational skills (Aim 7) as well. It might also serve to make the point that it might be fun to work behind the counter in a French shop for a bit (Aim 2).

The homework will need time to explain. Also, since our pupils cannot take their course-books home, we had better ensure they correctly copy down the key words before they leave. Since we shall inevitably be losing either some of our pair-work or the listening comprehension which would help to consolidate the vocabulary, we had better check particularly carefully that our weaker pupils are clear which word corresponds to which commodity. We had better leave rather more than five minutes for all this, for if it is hastily done the homework will be unsatisfactory and the result dispiriting.

This leaves us something over a quarter of an hour for handing back work, listening to the dialogues and two pieces of pair work. We will be brief about handing back work, concentrating on one or two points only and aiming to spend no more than five to seven minutes, leaving anything that cannot easily be dealt with in that time.

Something, however, still has to go. This is regrettable as both the listening comprehension and the pair work are characteristically communicative activities. Maybe the best solution is to postpone the listening comprehension until a subsequent lesson (not necessarily the next) as revision and consolidation. Active work such as pair work has to be done straight away after presentation of the material if it is to be successful. A sensible arrangement might be to give the class as long as they want for the first pair-work activity (straightforward shopping dialogue) relegating the second activity to the status of a dispensable or compressible filler to be used or omitted, or given only to certain quicker pairs according to what time allows. There will, after all, be plenty of opportunity to use this activity in other purchasing situations later if it is not used, or only briefly used, today. Identification of a compressible or dispensable filler which can be extended or abandoned in this way is a valuable aid to flexible timing. This item needs to be placed near the end of the lesson, but need not be the final activity which, as in this case, may be something crucial which we cannot afford to skimp.

There remains the question of when one hands back the previous piece of work or, in general, deals with minor administration or other tasks not integral to the present lesson. The obvious solution is to do it at the beginning and get it out of the way (as well as avoiding the danger of forgetting it) especially if it is something that can be dealt with very briefly. Against this, however, especially if the task is a bit more substantial, one may reasonably ask whether one really wants to fritter away the best minutes of the lesson, when the children are still fresh and eager, on administration or going over work. Possibly we might leave it until the end for then at least the bell will prevent discussion from dragging on. But today there is homework to set so at the end of the lesson one needs to have the class thinking about the new work, rather than the old. Straight after the discussion of the picture would obviously be the wrong moment. After a period of quite demanding teacher-centred work it is time to let them off the hook and work with each other for a bit. So it has to be after the pair work and before we come on to writing down what has to be written down for the homework. That way the books will be out ready on their desks and will not need to be scrabbled after twice.

So one's final list of activities will be approximately as follows:

1. Discussion of picture and presentation of vocabulary — 10–15 minutes
2. Pair work – shopping. J'ai/je n'ai pas kept in reserve for quick pairs if necessary — 7 minutes
3. Going over previous work — 7 minutes
4. Setting homework, checking necessary knowledge, copying down essential material. — 7–10 minutes
5. Allow to start homework — 3 minutes

Item 5 is a flexible item which need not be given at all, or may take up as much as five minutes. The advantage of allowing homework to be started in class is that a number of important queries, misunderstandings or other problems may not become apparent until the pupils attempt to put pen to paper.

Hopefully, the above will not have made the business of lesson planning seem too laborious and time consuming. In reality it is not so. Those who have been long in the profession sort these things out tacitly in the twinkling of an eye, and probably could not even tell us the thought processes that enable them to produce satisfying, stress-free and well-ordered lessons day after day. For others of us, the giving of some thought to the order of our activities enables lesson time to be used more effectively without adding more than a few minutes of preparation.

The above is not intended to imply that there is only one way to order a particular set of activities but to show that the order and emphasis given to various activities are under the teacher's control. They may therefore be arranged to best advantage rather than being determined by some preconceived plan or the chance order in which they come to mind.

PUPILS' RECORDS AND NOTE-TAKING

Part of the teacher's planning will be to decide what pupils should have down in their books as a permanent record. This will be particularly important where pupils do not keep a textbook of their own, or where the teacher makes use of a good deal of extra material or activities not suggested by the book. Writing for the record, even direct copying from the blackboard, provides a change of activity and contributes to pupils' familiarity with the written language. The careful recording of work covered is a satisfying activity and helps to reassure the child, as well as parents and anyone who may have cause to see pupils' books, that regular progress is being made. Ideally, this purpose may be served by the final version of pupils' writing tasks but sometimes it may be appropriate to give examples of dialogues, structures, ways of expressing certain functions or even individual words provided these are not written as lists with one-to-one English equivalents.

A brief routine period of writing at the end of each lesson is settling, and provides the teacher with a breathing-space in which to prepare for an orderly dismissal, start thinking about the next lesson, or brace himself for the dash to the car-park and the journey to the other site. Some teachers will wish pupils to make their own notes, writing down only those things they think they may otherwise forget. No doubt this is a useful discipline if carried out concientiously. At all costs, however, it is important to avoid the practice of making notes during the teacher's exposition or other activities. This simply becomes a way of withdrawing from participation and creates the illusion that what is written down need not be remembered.

HOMEWORK

There has been some debate about the value and use of home-work (Beattie 1987) and even some suggestion (White 1973: 69–72) that pupils would benefit more from interacting with their families or socialising with their friends rather than spending the best part of most evenings on tasks that could just as well be done at school. Reasonable amounts of homework, however, need not be onerous, often have the advantage of involving parents and give pupils an opportunity to organise themselves and take responsibility for their own learning. Provided work set is carefully explained and the amount is not excessive, homework also provides a valuable extension of learning time. Where pupils can be encouraged to work together on their homework this has the added advantage of promoting discussion and the skills of cooperation. If homework is to be set, it needs to be set regularly and in regular amounts, for if the pupils are to learn to organise their own lives and work they must be able to make some prediction of the demands that will be made upon them.

From a planning point of view the task is not to 'find something to give them' for homework but, from a series of valid learning tasks, to select those which, with proper preparation and instruc-tion, can best be done out of school. Homework is to be seen as an integral part of the learning programme, not something to be thought of on the spur of the moment, after the bell has gone. There is no reason why the whole lesson should not be planned in such a way as to enable pupils to make the best possible use of the following homework slot.

ASSESSMENT, FORMAL AND INFORMAL

The great advantage of specifying one's objectives in terms of what it is intended that the pupil should be able to do is that one can then check to find out whether they can in fact do it. As an educational model this is doubtless inadequate, for in a rich learning environment pupils will learn many things that have not been specifically envisaged (Wringe 1988: 9–13). Nevertheless, effective teaching at least implies that a good proportion of the skills and information that one has intended to pass on have in fact been learned by the majority of one's pupils.

At the end of units or longer periods of work many teachers will plan fairly formal periods of assessment. The purpose of this is not to identify future geniuses or provide ourselves with a set of failing marks as a rationing device or objective argument for debarring some pupils from further study in the subject. It is unnecessary that our test should produce a standard distribution of scores over the full range from 0 to 100 per cent with a bulge around the middle. We are specifically concerned to find out whether or not the main things we have been trying to teach during the preceding period have been learned, and would hope that the majority of our scores will be at the upper end of the range. If they are not, our work may be pitched at the wrong level for the class. We may be failing to identify clearly and give appropriate emphasis to our main objectives. We may be failing to persist adequately with the least able, or even to involve them at all. Alternatively, the problem may lie not in our teaching but in our test which may not relate sufficiently closely to the material taught.

It is important that our assessments should be seen to preserve a due balance between the four language skills. If, in particular, the oral production skill is under-represented this will inevitably have the effect, well known to many older language teachers, of convincing pupils that, whatever the teacher may say, this aspect of the subject is relatively unimportant. One solution to the problem of testing this skill is to visibly build into the score an estimated mark for each pupil's oral performance in class during the unit. If this is thought unsatisfactory the class may be given a substantial piece of reading comprehension or listening for information in the laboratory while brief individual or group tests are given. Individuals may also be asked questions or given assessed role-play tasks to perform in a whole class situation. It is possible to administer tests of oral production in the laboratory, but the resulting marking task may be too time consuming for this to be a possibility as a routine procedure.

If we are not to alienate the majority of our pupils (contrary to Aims 5 and 6) it is important that tests should not be presented as a threatening experience, with sanctions of ridicule and loss of face for those who do not do well.

It is perhaps not strictly necessary for pupils to know that they are being tested or told in advance that this is about to happen. Such a subterfuge, however, seems to show scant respect for the dignity of sensible young people and passes up the opportunity of devoting both class and homework time to purposeful revision, reminding pupils of what has been covered and advising them to 'pretest' themselves on the main tasks and give themselves some extra practice where necessary.

A more positive approach is to promote a sense of solidarity and involvement by presenting the test as a way of seeing how, as a group, we are progressing and whether we need to plan our work differently in future.

There is, however, no reason why pupils should not be given a numerical mark, letter grade or some other kind of evaluation of their individual progress. Equally, however, there is little justification for compiling and even less for publishing or formally reading out any kind of rank order. Whatever one's general views about the educational value of competition, many of our most effective teaching methods these days depend on cooperation and mutual support rather than individual effort in isolation.

Testing, often of an informal kind, also has its role to play within the economy of an individual lesson. The teacher's knowledge that he will test himself at the end of the period concentrates the mind wonderfully and acts as a powerful motivation to ensure that the time is spent actually doing things that will produce learning rather than simply occupying one's class or 'performing' before them as if the teacher's role were somehow akin to that of the actor or entertainer. In individual lessons the process of checking that one has successfully taught what one set out to teach will normally be brief, informal and often unperceived by the class. It may take the form of something to be written down by everyone, but equally it may take the form of a judiciously posed question giving little help in the framing of an answer and directed towards one of the least able members of the class. If he or she is able to provide a satisfactory reply we may be reasonably confident that others would also have done so.

SELF-EVALUATION AND RECORD-KEEPING

Like formal lesson planning there is a tendency to regard self-evaluation and record-keeping, other than in the form of a 'mark book', as something appropriate to students in initial training only. Certainly the keeping of a detailed and thoughtful file is a valuable training procedure, and established teachers may quite properly feel that to spend substantial amounts of time on this activity is unneccessary. Nevertheless, the keeping of brief notes or records is seen as an appropriate part of the work of many professionals these days, both for the sake of continuity when the 'client' is permanently or temporarily passed on to another professional, or for the purposes of review should problems arise or questions be raised. Arguably the very least teachers ought to do – and doubtless many do considerably more – is to make a brief dated note of how the lesson has been spent, as a point of reference for future planning and assessment.

Teaching is basically a sessional activity, and if today's lesson has been at all successful it is likely to be recycled for use on future occasions. It is therefore expedient to give a moment's reflection to how successful it has been, and to any problems and difficulties that might have been avoided. The likely alternative to such a critical review is to blunder and fudge one's way through the same imperfect performance time after time.

It is also desirable to review the success of each lesson as a preliminary to planning the next. If a projected activity was not completely successful, or one's informal testing revealed that one's lesson objectives had not been achieved, one clearly ought not to simply press on with the next exercise in the book, or even the highly original and stimulating activity that occurred to one at the weekend, as if all were going according to plan. Some revision or other remedial activity may need to be planned and undertaken before moving on. One's group may be finding the work less demanding than one had anticipated, or their earlier enthusiasm, that one had begun to take for granted, may unexpectedly have begun to wane.

These processes of review, reflection and the adjustment of both methods and goals are not peculiar to the planning of lessons or, indeed, to education, but are essential features of rational planning in any field.

REVIEW AND ENHANCEMENT

1. Review all parts of the main course-book used in your school together.
   (a) List the topics covered and note any omission in the light of your school's GCSE syllabus.
   (b) Identify the main types of learning activity suggested and the changing balance of activities from stage to stage.
   (c) Consider in greater detail the course for one of the years in which you teach. Make an estimate of the approximate time required for each unit and note a provisional starting date for each.
   (d) Note any imbalance in the treatment of the four language skills and consider ways of remedying this.
   (e) Note any units which seem particularly interesting or fertile and any which seem thin, too difficult or likely to be thought 'silly' by your pupils. Consider what strategies you will use for dealing with these problems when they arise.
   (f) Note any recurring activities or pattern of activities that may help to give regularity and structure to your work on the various units.
2. Attempt to reconstruct your teaching of a recent unit.
   (a) List what you take to have been the main objectives of the unit. Say what attempts you made to ascertain whether they had been achieved.

(b) Take any objective individually and say what proportion of your pupils you think achieved it. Take five pupils at random and attempt to say which of the objectives each had achieved.

(c) Consider a future unit. Spend some time identifying and developing a possible culminating activity. Then plan work for the remainder of the unit.

3. Take a substantial piece of material – text, recording or picture – and

(a) Devise a series of activities arising from it to occupy approximately 60 minutes of class time.

(b) Amend and reschedule these to make best use of a 40 minute period plus homework.

(c) List your objectives and assumptions about the class and pupils' previous knowledge. Say how you will informally test that your objectives have been achieved.

FURTHER READING

Beattie N 1987 'Homework in the teaching and learning of modern languages, 11–16', *British Journal of Language Teaching*, **25** (2), 67–72

Davies I K 1976 *Objectives in Curriculum Design*, McGraw-Hill, Maidenhead

Perrott E 1982 *Effective Teaching*, Longman, London, pp. 12–20

CHAPTER 3

The receptive skills: listening and reading

The effects of the change to communicative language teaching are nowhere more apparent than in the changed attitude to the receptive skills of understanding the written and more especially the spoken word.

Traditionally, reading the foreign language was regarded as a kind of very rapid *sotto voce* translation. If one could do a good unseen, one would not have much difficulty with the comprehension test. Aural comprehension was simply a matter of recognising when read aloud those words and structures with which one was already familar in writing.

Such a view was, perhaps, not entirely surprising. Facilities for rapidly reproducing authentic written and printed ephemera or recorded speech have not long been available and, when travel abroad was less frequent, contact with the foreign language, if it continued after the fifth year, was through the literary medium. To this degree, reading Maupassant and Daudet was as valid a preparation for the future as being able to understand a snack-bar menu or a ferry announcement.

In the present educational situation in which language teachers must provide valid educational experience for pupils across the ability range the receptive skills are of particular importance. Productive skills, including that of translating into good English, are admirably suited to the task of creating failure. A simple prose or essay riddled with mistakes is clearly an educational achievement of no value and its producer unequivocally labelled as unsuitable for academic study.

By contrast, any degree of understanding of speech or writing in the foreign tongue is an identifiable achievement, showing that the pupil has either learned something or managed to work something out for himself. Besides being valid at the lower end of the ability range it is also capable of stretching the most able, for both texts and utterances in the foreign language, as in the mother tongue, may exhibit every degree of complexity and subtlety ranging from the waiter's answer to an enquiry about the price of beer to the precise meaning of the hero's more difficult speeches in *Faust*, Part II.

AUTHENTIC MATERIALS AND TASKS

Since the receptive skills are now obviously important and may occupy well over half of the class's time, it is essential that this part of the work should be thoroughly effective and stimulating. A string of unconnected multiple-choice reading comprehension exercises or aural comprehensions taken over from the previous regime, and handled with little conviction of their importance will not meet the bill. Such exercises fail to stretch and stimulate the ablest and those with the most enquiring minds, and may also leave the less able and interested unmoved and floundering.

The least that is required is that the materials with which pupils work, particularly in the earlier stages and with less academically ambitious groups, should be things that they could – now or in the foreseeable future – conceivably want or need to understand for the achievement of purposes they might plausibly wish to achieve. Consequently a supply of varied, stimulating and appropriate authentic materials is the *sine qua non* of effective teaching. Established courses may, and increasingly must, provide a good range of these if they are to achieve credibility, but often they will need to be supplemented. This in turn implies a need for good, convenient arrangements for collecting, reproducing and storing supplementary material. Here, as in other aspects of teaching, effectiveness may be as much a matter of good management as of the classroom performance of individual teachers.

As regards the range of appropriate materials for listening comprehension there exists something of a minor controversy between the more purist devotees of authenticity and those who take a slightly more liberal view. On the narrow interpretation, audio recordings are supposed only to be appropriate when the listener would not actually be able to see the speaker: public announcements over the loudspeaker, telephone conversations, sound-broadcast items such as weather forecasts and presumably such conversations as may be supposed to take place in the dark. In all other situations, so the argument goes, the listener has the advantage of such non-verbal clues as facial expression and gesture, and often as well the presence of the objects being talked about. Possibly such arguments are valuable in promoting the use of film and video. The arrival of these facilities in every classroom is as yet some way off, however, and production costs may limit their widespread availability indefinitely. In the meantime it would be unfortunate if the above arguments were to inhibit the relatively cheap and convenient use of audio-cassette recordings or serve educational authorities as a justification for limiting expenditure on purely audio facilities.

In the mother tongue neither adults nor children appear to experience particular difficulty in following sound broadcasts or recordings of talks, or conversations. We do not need to look at the person speaking to us all the time in order to understand him or her, and if it is courteous to do so, this is in order to provide feedback to the speaker, so that he or she knows how we are responding to his or her words, rather than for the sake of our own better comprehension.

It would therefore seem highly desirable that copious use should continue to be made, for both classroom and individual work (Robins 1986), of simple sound recordings of authentic talk. The only requirement is that this should be talk of a kind likely to be encountered by an English visitor. Explanations, instructions, replies to enquiries and the exchange of courtesies and personal information between newly made acquaintances are particularly appropriate. It is helpful if not only our materials but also the tasks we set our pupils bear the stamp of authenticity. This concern, however, should not be exaggerated to the point of absurdity. It is certainly not wrong for any class ever to study a menu without going through the charade of ordering a meal, or to fill in multiple-choice boxes unless they are likely to be faced with a set of buttons to press in real life. To insist on such a degree of authenticity is to confuse competence (see Chomsky 1965: 3–14) with performance in a particularly crass way.

Our concern as teachers is with competence, with enabling pupils to do a range of things with language at some point in the future, should the occasion arise. We cannot exactly predict every situation our pupils are likely to encounter abroad nor, if we wish them to be able to respond intelligently and flexibly, should we attempt to do so.

This said, there is nevertheless wisdom in the observation that in real life successful reading or listening is often not followed by the writing or the giving of answers designed simply to test whether or not one has understood. If it is followed by speaking this will often be in the form of making some choice, or perhaps some further enquiry. As often as not, however, one's response will not be answering at all, but doing something. Having asked directions, enquired the whereabouts of certain buildings or services, asked after the availability or price of certain goods, enquired whether or not a seat is available and so on, one simply goes where one is directed, presses the appropriate knob or inserts one's coin, sits down or looks for another seat elsewhere. Any verbal response one makes will often be no more than a conventional expression of thanks. One may perhaps write down the time of a train or the price of a ticket for convenience, but the essential thing is that one returns to the station at the correct hour, or hands over the appropriate banknotes.

Considerations of time and space mean that these conditions cannot be reproduced in the classroom, and it cannot be pretended that the consequences of getting into the wrong train in imagination bear any resemblance to those of doing so in reality. Nevertheless, for some pupils there will be appeal and attraction in the fact that correctly comprehending the printed text or recorded utterance is supposed to contribute to the performance of a practical task. It will be an added bonus that the comprehension of even fairly difficult material can be demonstrated in a relatively non-verbal manner. Though the task of comprehension may be every bit as intellectually stretching as that of production, it is often *experienced* as easier and certainly less stressful by many pupils if no public verbal performance is required.

It is true that some imaginative teachers and course-book writers have devised materials in which comprehension leads on to practical activity, the actual doing or making of things. Some course-books contain a recipe or two on the assumption that an occasional room-swap with home economics can be arranged and instructions for making kites and folding cardboard models also occur and may even be used from time to time.

No doubt there is potential for action research in the idea of combining foreign language teaching with practical subjects. As a staple procedure, however, ticking the right box, writing down the key letter, marking a plan or diagram or, at most, writing down an appropriate word – the name of a shop, service or product, for example, may simply have to stand for the action that would be taken in real life. That the tasks we ask our pupils to perform do in fact stand for actions rather than simply answers for teachers to mark can, however, often be made clear without exposing ourselves too obviously to caricature. No harm is done if our multiple-choice boxes do sometimes look rather like the buttons in the lift taking us to various floors of a department store, the numbered doors of classrooms down the corridor of our imaginary *collège* or a row of buses about to depart for various destinations.

MODES OF READING AND LISTENING

Traditionally, teachers have recognised only one kind of reading: that which was careful and painstaking and as a result of which one understood every word. Skipping and guessing were certainly frowned upon and failure to check an unfamiliar word in the dictionary, even when its meaning seemed fairly obvious, was regarded as careless and idle. Certainly, such thorough, careful reading is a skill which ought not to be lost and no doubt it is a valuable study tool, especially in languages.

But there are other less demanding and equally valid modes of reading. All may need to be practised if they are to be efficiently acquired. How good readers read will depend on the purpose for which they are reading. We certainly do not read for pleasure in the same way as we scrutinise the small print of an insurance document or idly glance through publicity material before dismissing it as being of no interest to us. One may skim for gist, or scan for specific information while leaving the remainder of the text virtually unread. Odd words which are unfamiliar will certainly not detain us, or even whole sentences whose structure is too complicated, once we have assured ourselves that they are not essential to what we are trying to find out. Whole paragraphs may be passed over or filtered out if the first few phrases indicate that they are not important or their content can easily be anticipated.

The practice of engaging pupils in reading and listening for immediate practical purposes marks an important change of emphasis away from the more general 'knowledge of the whole language' aimed at in former times. It nevertheless remains a perfectly proper aim that our pupils should participate fully in more general conversations, rather than simply seeking to pick out such information as is relevant to their immediate purposes. By the same token we not only wish pupils to learn to read for information in order to know which door to go through and so on, but also for interest and pleasure. No doubt, the extended reading done in the past was too often of a literary narrative kind. Clearly much of the material read for pleasure and interest outside the classroom is less earnest and more ephemeral: newspaper and magazine articles, non-fiction books on non-academic topics, spicy anecdotes, romantic fiction, comic strips and so on. A good deal of increasingly accessible narrative, including narrative aimed at the teenage age-group, also exists in all of the foreign languages commonly studied. Despite any reservations we might feel about endorsing commercialised pop culture it is difficult to believe that great harm is done if someone who enjoys light reading in his own tongue is led to find a source of similar enjoyment in the foreign language.

If this view is accepted then the effective teaching of reading must include not only developing the *skills* of extended reading, but also the *habit* of reading for interest and pleasure in the foreign language, even when the reading in question has not been set as a specific assignment. The provision of expendable reading material for a whole school necessarily poses a resources problem. The practice of encouraging pupils to buy foreign language magazines and other educational supplements from their own pockets is a controversial one, though one that may well become increasingly widespread. Certainly some provision on a library or reading-room basis in the school is essential so that those pupils who show a particular interest may be encouraged, and at least see that such materials exist. Something equivalent to the English departments 'library period' in which class time is provided for relatively unstructured reading is also a possibility.

The use of readers of a more traditional kind has virtually disappeared, yet when readers of a suitable level are provided they are avidly read by some pupils. As this kind of voluntary reading largely takes place in the pupils' own time and is often carried on with more intensity than many classroom activities it would appear to be a highly profitable activity to encourage. There is therefore good reason to budget for the provision of a suitable supply of readers, and building in a regular time for the lending and keeping track of readers and similar items into each class's scheme of work.

Extended listening on a similar basis would seem equally desirable. Taking advantage of the widespread availability of cassette recorders in the homes of many pupils and the existence of fast multi-copying facilities some schools (Robins 1986) have experimented with the setting of listening comprehension homework and the issue of language recordings on a library basis. It must be said, however, that no great supply of good, interesting material is available in the aural medium. Genuinely authentic material in the foreign language is normally too hard for any but the most advanced school students. Off-air recordings of school language broadcasts and some commercially produced dialogues and short dramatisations may appeal on an interest basis to enthusiastic pupils, and for this reason the possibilities of such library provision ought to be explored.

THE COMPREHENSION PROCESS

So far we have been largely concerned with the question of *what* it is desirable for our pupils to learn to comprehend, rather than how we should best go about the task of teaching them to do so. We have more or less assumed that, provided adequate practice is given in tasks bearing sufficient resemblance to real-life situations, the requisite abilities will be acquired.

Certainly the provision of a good balance of practice activity and sensibly graded material, efficiently organised and carried out under good motivational conditions, is the prime requirement of satisfactory progress. Some reflection about the nature of the comprehension process may, however, be helpful in arranging such practice to best advantage.

Though not a great deal is known about this process or how best to teach it, some of the few things that are known are relatively helpful. Perhaps the most important of these is that the term 'decoding' used as a technical term by some psychologists to refer to the process of receiving and interpreting communications in speech and writing, is somewhat misleading. To the layman this suggests a process of replacing a string of signs and symbols by something more immediately comprehensible before being in a position to 'read the message back'. Yet in fact this is certainly not how we proceed when we read or listen to something in a foreign language.

In many situations, language – speech, public notices, print, etc. – will be present as one element among others. Our response, the action we take or the replies we make, reflect our grasp of the situation as a whole, rather than simply our literal understanding of any words that may be said or written. We take a general overview of the situation before turning to details. The same applies when we turn our attention to the linguistic element itself. We proceed heuristically by hypothesis and falsification. What sort of a message is this? A narrative report perhaps? Or information about a resort? Or instructions? Is the speaker or writer inviting, threatening or just attempting to inform us. Only when this process of general orientation is complete do we begin to concentrate on the specifics of what is being said, and often we do not even reach this point. We become aware that we know enough. The message, or this section of the message, is not relevant to our purposes and we dismiss it from the centre stage of our attention.

Much of the information we make use of in this process is tacit. Contextually important cues quickly recede below the threshold of our consciousness if, indeed, they ever rose above it. We know without explicitly taking note of the fact that, for example,

This is a rather up-market restaurant. We cannot simply march in and order Pepsi and a bag of frites.

The man is angry and is speaking ironically. When he says 'Je suis un sot, je suppose', we are not expected to smile and agree.

The event being described happened some time ago. It will be courteous to nod, and show interest, but no action will be required. The details are not important.

Substantial parts of what we hear or read will be rhetorical in their intention. A newspaper article may contain a number of sentences packed with facts and figures. This information is not required by the reader but is intended to convey the message:

'The writer has done his research and can be believed' (Girard 1986: 50–2).

Much of what we read, and more especially of what we hear is redundant. It does not have to be there and if it *is* there it does not have to be retained for the message to be understood perfectly. Sometimes the redundancy is inherent in the syntax of the language.

'John paused. He took his handkerchief from his pocket and blew his nose.' The 'he' and the thrice-repeated 'his' are unnecessary and, in some languages, would not occur. Some people might think that the whole first clause of the second sentence is unnecessary. Its purpose is not to convey information, but to create the impression that John is acting slowly and with deliberation.

Speech contains much paraphrase and repetition, both for emphasis and to give the listener time to process and absorb what is being said. Its purpose may be to keep the conversation going or simply hold the floor. The speaker has not yet decided what to say next, but he wishes to prevent others from interrupting. The efficient listener filters out much of the redundant material and that which is not relevant to his purposes. If he does not he is simply overwhelmed and loses the thread of what is being said in a mass of detail.

Redundancy is also present in writing, though to a much smaller degree. Good writing is reasonably concise and avoids obvious repetition. Allowing for 'processing time' is more or less unnecessary as the reader controls the speed at which the message is received, and can refer back or reread if he needs to. Terse or deliberately concise writing in which every word counts, however, is uncomfortable and difficult to read. The differences between writing and speech mean that narrative or other material intended to be read is inappropriate for practice in oral comprehension. It also explains why made-up or edited dialogues often fall short of complete authenticity.

From what has been said it will be clear that the comprehension of speech and writing is by no means a passive process in which the words simply fall upon a *tabula rasa* or are registered on some kind of recording medium. What is understood will depend as much on what the recipient brings to the situation as on what is actually said or written. What he brings will be both his knowledge of the world and his familiarity with the language. This knowledge enables him to anticipate what he is about to hear or read (Abbott and Wingard 1981: 61–2).

For example, knowledge of the options normally offered one at cinemas, clothes shops or filling-stations or the kind of information provided by guidebooks or weather forecasts greatly limits the possible range of what is about to be heard. As regards the listener's linguistic knowledge, many words have as part of their function to signal clearly what is to come next. In English 'since . . .' often signals a reason for the main part of the sentence but warns us that this main part will not be heard until the since-clause is complete. 'However', signals a contradiction of what has gone before and 'Although . . .' a reservation. Knowledge of the polite conventions surrounding invitations enables us to predict that, spoken in a certain tone, the words 'I'd love to come up and see your etchings' will be followed by a polite excuse, whereas 'Well, I don't normally even *speak* to strange men . . .' will probably be followed by a modest acceptance.

Prediction of what one is about to hear or read means that one need only give what follows enough of one's attention to confirm that one's expectations are being fulfilled. It is no longer necessary to attempt to interpret every sound that falls upon the ear, or every mark on the paper. The processing task is greatly simplified and, in the case of both listening and reading, the load on short-term memory greatly reduced, for it appears that what is immediately heard or read must be held in the short-term memory until the general import of the message is grasped, this general import then being held in the longer-term memory. This is why we are usually able to remember the gist of what we hear or read, provided we are able to make sense of it, rather than being able to recall it verbatim. It appears that both the process of anticipating and that of holding in the short-term memory are less efficient in a newly acquired language than in the mother tongue (Abbott and Wingard 1981: 60–3).

This does not mean that speech intended for listening comprehension should be artificially slowed down, for this in itself may distort the natural rhythms and connections and may actually render the task of understanding more difficult. However, slightly longer gaps between utterances to allow processing to take place may be helpful, as may some slight stressing of those words and phrases that serve as clues to what is about to follow, provided this is not carried to excess.

DEVELOPING THE RECEPTIVE SKILLS

If we accept the above account of what happens when we comprehend speech or writing, certain things follow for our practice in teaching this skill. The first of these is that comprehension, both listening and reading, is a skill of its own and will not just happen as a result of some general knowledge of the language. It is not sufficient to possess a certain stock of vocabulary and a knowledge of the main rules of syntax. Nor is it the case that if we can speak or write the language we are bound to be able to understand it, on the grounds that we could hardly say things we could not understand. For we can make ourselves understood with a relatively limited stock of language, whereas when we attempt to comprehend, we are exposed to the full range of language the speaker or writer throws at us. Sympathetic or not, the native speaker may well not be conscious of the limits of our understanding, especially if the few things we ourselves say are idiomatic and confidently expressed.

Though skill in comprehension cannot be acquired without a great deal of specific practice of that skill itself in situations resembling those likely to be met in real life, it does not follow that all the time we are able to spend on that aspect of language learning should be totally devoted to authentic problem-solving activities. It is widely recognized by teachers in many areas of activity that practice alone is less effective than practice interspersed with explanation and comment. Addressing a full-blown authentic comprehension task is essentially a testing rather than a teaching activity. The distinction between the two ought not, perhaps, to be too sharply drawn for, of course, we may learn a great deal from doing tests of one kind and another. It may not, however, be entirely productive to set pupils multiple-choice exercises, 'At the filling-station' or 'In the department store', unless much of the significant language involved has already been met in some sort of teacher-centred discussion, explication or other fairly supportive mode in which pupils' tentative hypotheses about meaning can be quickly confirmed or falsified.

Skimming, scanning and other forms of reading for information are no doubt skills which must be explicitly acquired and practised. It is also the case, as our comments on redundancy and other aspects of understanding linguistic material make clear, that it is perfectly appropriate and highly desirable that pupils attempt these activities without a prior knowledge of all the lexis or all the syntax involved. Much new vocabulary and syntax will come to be understood in the process itself. Some need not be known or taken cognisance of at all on this occasion or at this stage. Some, indeed, may not even need to be known by foreign speakers of the language at all. Such activities, however, cannot take place and must lead to demoralisation and guessing on a pot-luck basis without previous knowledge of a good proportion of the language involved. Effective teaching of the comprehension skills therefore certainly involves adequate practice. Equally essential, however, are careful grading, adequate preparation and the giving of sufficient feedback.

Our understanding of the process by which comprehension takes place clearly suggests that any form of translating from the foreign language will be inadequate, either as a means of bringing about an understanding of a particular text, or as a means of more generally developing comprehension skills. This will come as no surprise to those who experienced a traditional A-level literature course in which they had to translate French literature set books word for word or, more likely, sat through double period after double period while they were being translated by the teacher. Such a process often left one with as little real comprehension of what Phèdre or Mephistopheles were saying as before the lesson. Translation may fail to ensure comprehension of the message. Conversely, knowing the mother-tongue equivalent of every word is often unnecessary to a very full understanding of what is being read or heard.

The above goes not only for translation into the mother tongue but equally for any approach based on word-for-word explication, including explication or paraphrase in the foreign language. The more fruitful approach must be to encourage the natural tendency to take cognisance of the context as a whole and attempt to gain a general overview before homing in on matters of detail. The habit of concentrating on individual words may inhibit this normal response and pupils may become so alarmed by one or two unfamiliar words that they all too easily convince themselves that they understand nothing at all. This may occur even though the words in question may be redundant to the comprehension task in which they are engaged, or readily deducible from the context.

It is possible to identify two distinct approaches to the task of teaching comprehension. On the one hand, one may take the view that we know so little about the process by which comprehension takes place that the most sensible thing to do is simply to provide plenty of carefully graded practice with discussion and feedback. Provided the proportion of new to familiar material is relatively low, pupils will no doubt devise their own strategies for coping, and gradually increase the range of vocabulary and structure with which they are familiar.

Alternatively, one may adopt a more analytical approach, attempting to develop the various skills involved in aural and reading comprehension (Abbott and Wingard 1981: 66–9). One may, for example, attempt to improve pupils' aural discrimination between individual sounds or develop their ability to recognise known words among others.

Teachers may also attempt to develop the skill of anticipation, so that the 'receiver' has less processing work to do and simply needs to monitor what follows at a relatively low level of attention, to check that his anticipation has been correct. This may be done using the relatively formal exercise of completing unfinished sentences or short passages. Cloze exercises are one variety of this exercise. The pupil is required, from his knowledge of the language, to anticipate the word that would occur (or deduce which word would have occurred) in the space. The more easily he is able to do this, the more apparent it is that he is able to comprehend the message without actually taking cognisance of every single word.

At a more informal level one may seek to develop powers of anticipation by drawing attention to various 'signal' words such as *d'abord, ensuite, da, obgleich, schon . . . aber*, etc. In the first place these highly important words for the general sense and structure of a text may simply not be known. But even when the mother-tongue equivalent can be produced pupils may still form little notion of the likely general sense of what is to follow.

There is, of course, no contradiction between providing copious practice and giving due attention to specific aspects of the comprehension task as the necessity for this becomes apparent. Like successful sports coaches and other teachers of skilled activities we shall no doubt attempt to achieve a judicious mix of specific coaching and more unstructured practice. In the field of comprehension more than in other aspects of language learning, however, there may seem to be a danger that talk of skills may lead us to concentrate on repetitive practice, forgetting that most worthwhile skills have a substantial cognitive element.

REVIEW AND ENHANCEMENT

1. Consider one or two units you have recently taught in the third or fourth years.
   (a) List the activities and materials whose prime purpose was to develop the reading and listening skills.
   (b) Consider the adequacy of these in terms of both quantity and level. Do they sufficiently extend pupils' ability to comprehend beyond the level of their productive use of the language.
   (c) If possible, obtain a longer or more difficult piece of material on a similar topic. Transform this into a comprehension test by means of a small number of simple true or false questions in English. Give this to your class with an adequate allowance of time to enable them to complete the questions. In the light of their performance, consider again whether your pupils are adequately extended by your present material. If necessary consider how your material might be supplemented.
   NB. You should carefully explain the purpose of this exercise to the class before it is administered and provide some general indication of the content of the passage or recording.

2. Review the work of one of your classes in years two, three or four over the period of about a month and bring together the material intended for reading comprehension.
   (a) Attempt to decide whether each of these pieces of material is appropriate for developing full or detailed comprehension, reading for gist or scanning for information. Note any systematic imbalances.
   (b) Consider reading comprehension materials to be used by the same group in the next two units. If previous imbalances persist, consider how the materials may be supplemented or the projected activities modified.
3. Take a piece of recorded material which does not form part of a course currently being used by you, and consider its potential as material for developing listening comprehension.
   (a) Decide whether it is most suitable for full, detailed comprehension or listening for gist or information. If the latter, identify parts which do not have to be understood.
   (b) Provisionally devise ways of testing comprehension of the appropriate kind.
   (c) Review these with a view to making them more authentic, amusing or imaginative.
   (d) Decide what preparation or introduction would be necessary in order to ensure that pupils obtain maximum benefit and satisfaction from the activity.
   If possible find a suitable time to try out your material with one of your classes. Note the success of your material and the response of your class. Compare this with results normally achieved with materials provided in your course. Attempt to account for any differences.
4. Take a piece of reading or listening comprehension material which you intend to use in the near future.
   (a) Consider aspects of this such as title, illustrations, format, background noises, tone of voice, etc. which enable pupils to make preliminary predictions regarding the content of the material. Analyse for linguistic predictors such as introductory remarks, conjunctions, interjections or other discourse markers.
   (b) Discuss the material with the class, encouraging them to interpret the various predictors before reading or listening to the whole text.
5. Review arrangements and resources for reading and listening for interest in the school.
   (a) Discuss the adequacy and use made of these with colleagues.
   (b) Identify one limited and specific way in which the situation can be improved during the next half-term.

FURTHER READING

Abbott G and Wingard P (eds) 1981 *The Teaching of English as an International Language*. Collins, London

Page B 1986 'Teaching listening skills for GCSE', in M Buckby *et al*, *Teaching Modern Languages for the GCSE*. British Association for Language Teaching, Modern Language Association, Leeds, pp. 3–19.

Robins J A 1986 'Hear! Hear! – an extension of listening comprehension', *British Journal of Language Teaching*, **19** (2), 93–7

SEC 1986 *French GCSE: A Guide for Teachers*. Open University Press, Milton Keynes

Ur P 1984 *Teaching Listening Comprehension*. Oxford University Press, London

CHAPTER 4

Speaking

PRESENTING THE LANGUAGE TASK

Part of the thinking behind the communicative approach to language teaching is that competence in language is a matter of appropriate behaviour in a particular situation. There are, that is, communicative rules for use without which the rules of grammar would be useless (Hymes 1972: 278). Appropriate linguistic behaviour is, among other things, a social skill which entails a proper grasp of the situation in which one's performance takes place.

This approach stands in sharp contrast to the somewhat mechanistic approach of the past, in which the pupil was required to produce formally correct but often entirely disembodied language, without much conception of when or how he might have the opportunity to use it in real life. To carefully locate the piece of language in a specific and authentic context in the appropriate country may, of course, contribute to the pupil's understanding of the culture and civilisation of the country (Aim 3) as well, hopefully, as encouraging a sympathetic approach to other cultures and civilisations generally (Aim 6). In addition it may contribute to their general social and personal education as well as providing some motivation and sense of relevance for the task in hand. An understanding of the situation to which the piece of language to be learned belongs is also an essential part of the skill of using that piece of language.

In support of what may seem the rather ambitious claims above, let us consider a unit of work which deals with enquiry about accommodation, booking a room in a hotel and so on. To the adult, middle-class language learner the situation is perfectly familiar. One has stayed in hotels in Winchester or York so that, apart from knowing about the *fiche de police* to be filled in, and remembering that breakfast is not included in the price, all one has to do in Poitiers or Lyons is to master the new sounds appropriate to presenting oneself at the reception, enquiring about single, double or family rooms, locking-up time, prices and so on. For some of our pupils, however, these activities will seem as much a part of their familiar reality as piloting Concorde or taking the salute at the Changing of the Guard.

Yet if our teaching is to have any validity at all, we must at

least suppose that at some time in their lives many of our pupils
will have occasion to put up in a hotel or lodgings both in Britain
and abroad. It is therefore not at all inappropriate to hash over
the situation with one's class to the point where they can
perfectly well imagine a person like themselves a few years hence
being in Poitiers or Lyons and having occasion to seek accommodation for the night, considering in what part of the town
hotels might be expected to be found, how one might make one's
initial choice, what one might wish to find out before booking in,
what options are likely to be offered one, and so on. Despite the
limitations of their actual experience one will, in point of fact,
not need to tell them a great deal. Thirteen-year-olds have
common sense as well as lively imaginations, and some of them
will enjoy giving us and their classmates the benefit of such
knowledge of the world as they may think they have. The process
need not take long.

As the course progresses it is most desirable that as much of
this discussion as possible should take place in the foreign
language. Nevertheless, the purpose of this part of the lesson is
to help pupils become involved and come to feel at home in the
situation to which the new piece of language belongs. The overriding requirement, therefore, is that they should feel able to
contribute their own comments in whatever language is being
used.

Once the class have instructed us in how to conduct ourselves
when booking into a hotel, they are in a position to make sense
of the first recorded dialogue or, failing this, to tell one in the
foreign language, what one needs to say, i.e. to begin composing
the first collective dialogue. The result will probably not be an
incredibly suave enquiry or booking and will certainly recycle a
good deal of language learned in other contexts.

It is therefore essential that at some fairly early stage they
should either hear or at least read a model dialogue and incorporate the new linguistic material it contains. But this should not
happen too soon, for the impression one hopes to create is that,
if one has one's wits about one, there is not much to this business
of booking into a hotel and that one knew most of it already. For
it is important that our pupils should not only acquire the
language needed to score in the GCSE role-play, but should
develop confidence in their ability to tackle this and other
language tasks in the future.

INTRODUCING NEW LANGUAGE

Once pupils have become involved in a particular situation and
begun to confront its linguistic requirements, it is important to
judge the right moment to feed in new material. One way of

doing this was indicated in the previous section. In all the current enthusiasm for new communicative approaches and classroom techniques to practise communicative skills, however, not much thought has been given to the question of how best to present new material. Pair work, group work, classroom surveys, communication-gap exercises and so on are essentially designed to develop skill, confidence and ingenuity in the use of language one already partly possesses, rather than for confronting and absorbing language that was previously unfamiliar.

As the course progresses much new vocabulary and idiom will naturally be absorbed incidentally as it occurs among other language which is already known. Particularly in the early stages, however, pupils will periodically meet new language functions or a whole range of new vocabulary which must first be understood and then acquired reasonably accurately before being practised in a more fluid and less controlled situation.

If not much thought has been given to the question of expositional techniques appropriate to the progressive approach implied by current syllabuses and course materials, this is no doubt because exposition as such, that is the deliberate and controlled presentation of new material and concepts, tends to be shied away from as didactic or unduly teacher-centred. In consequence, when new material has to be presented this may be done in crude archaic ways which contrast starkly with the spirit of the new approach being followed the rest of the time. Otherwise progressive and enlightened teachers may suddenly revert to the giving of lists of necessary words and expressions with their English equivalents. A number of widely used courses, apparently committed to a more up-to-date and professional approach, also present new material in this way, or simply allow this aspect of the class's work to go by default. Consequently, many pupils may be left in the dark about what is meant, or have to make of the lesson what they can.

If new language is not specifically identified, presented and consolidated in an accurate form pupils will certainly learn to 'get by' (in class though less obviously so in the real world) with their previous knowledge, mangled or restricted versions of the new material and various 'communication strategies', including non-linguistic ones suggested by the various examination boards.

Though the value of these strategies is not denied they should be seen as a supplement, not as a substitute for a satisfactory knowledge of requisite structure and lexis. Those who see many language classes being taught cannot, indeed, be unaware of the development among pupils and teachers of a kind of 'Français de petit Anglais' for use in certain rather stereotyped communicative classroom activities. The precise form of this collective interlanguage would prove an interesting linguistic study in its own right. Its development has no doubt been encouraged by the suggestion that grammatical and other unorthodoxies are significant only if they actually prevent the message from being understood, and should therefore not be interfered with.

Certainly, communication should be the first priority and due credit given for its achievement, however primitive and insolite the means employed. But it is only a minimal achievement. The ultimate aim is communication which is confident, flexible, unambiguous and does not provoke ridicule, or require too many concessions from the hearer. If this aim is to be achieved, communicative activities will often need to be prepared for with sound precommunicative (Littlewood 1981: 8–9) presentation, practice and rehearsal.

Let us suppose we are concerned to teach the language necessary for getting a drink or a snack in a French café. Hopefully our lesson will culminate in some such communicative activity as the following. Pupils are divided into groups of five. Taking turns in the various roles one member of the group asks three of the others what they would like and relays the whole order, including his own choice to the fifth member of the group who, as waiter, confirms the order and tots up the price. By way of development this simple scenario can no doubt be complicated by changes of mind after the addition has been made, the fact that certain items listed on the menu are unavailable, wrong items are bought and sent back, bills incorrectly calculated and have to be courteously challenged, and so on.

Both in real life and in the classroom the original simple situation could no doubt take place with relatively little firm grasp of the relevant vocabulary or appropriate idiom, provided the menu remains available as (some will no doubt point out) it would in real life. However hesitantly or imperfectly pronounced, the *café* and *limonade* will be fairly readily comprehensible to the sympathetic English classmate and much group work and pair work that goes on in language classrooms takes place on this basis.

Any self-respecting teenager, however, not only wants to get his doughnut or whatever, but do so with sufficient confidence and aplomb to create a good impression on his French companions. Successful performance of the task may not entail being mistaken for a native speaker, but the waiter should have no excuse to ask for constant repetition, break into his own imperfect English or snigger behind his hand. It is also desirable that the pupil should not only be able to use the relevant vocabulary and other linguistic formulae here and now in the classroom, but should retain them for future use.

The precommunicative practice and rehearsal necessary to this end has to be teacher-centred since the teacher must serve as the model or draw attention to key features if recorded material is used. He must also coach, criticise and insist on acceptable performance, and, of course, encourage. Techniques and principles fundamental to all effective teaching and widely applied in connection with earlier oral approaches to language teaching may be relevant here, but with significant adjustments to bring them as closely into line with a communicative methodology as possible.

Most recently published courses include flash-cards for presenting and practising the situation outlined above. In the absence of these, self-made cards or blackboard sketches are easily produced. Needless to say the key qualities of these and other visuals is economy, simplicity and immediate recognisability. The number of these should not be left to chance or inspiration. It must be sufficient to allow variety, so that pupils have the impression of giving a range of different answers, without repetition, but not so many as to turn the presentation into a memorisation chore. About five clearly identifiable and commonly required items is the right sort of number. A more extensive printed menu can be used later if it is thought desirable. It is not of course sufficient to present each item once, have it correctly identified by one bright pupil, repeated by the whole class and laid aside. The items are intended to be learned by all members of the class and this entails plenty of repetition, working with two or three cards intensively before introducing further ones.

Whereas, however, a teacher following a traditional oral approach requiring that pupils' replies should simply be meaningful and true would begin by asking 'Qu'est-ce que c'est?' to ensure identification of all items before proceeding to anything more complex it is, in fact, possible to be slightly more imaginative.

– Alors, nous sommes au café. – Je suis le garçon.
– Vous désirez, Monsieur? (To a good pupil.)
– Une limonade? (Display card.) Une glace? (Ditto.)
– Une limonade? (Nod, nod.) Oui?
– Bien, une limonade.
– Et vous, Mademoiselle? Vous désirez?
– Une limonade ou une glace? (Display ice-cream card.)

At this point well-known techniques of individual and class repetition are perfectly in order. The criticism that waiters do not authentically require their customers to chant their orders in unison is facetious and out of line.

New vocabulary can be introduced by means of alternative questions. 'Vous désirez une glace? Ou des frites?' (Show chips card.) This may seem slightly cumbersome, but is certainly smoother and more professional than writing *frites* on the board with its English equivalent. Displaying the chips card in this way enables the pupil to deduce that these things are called *frites*. They are certainly not *glace* for he already knows that *glace* is something else.

Pupils introduced to new vocabulary in this way will often assert that they have learnt nothing new, for since they are able to order 'des frites' without being told what they are, they assume they must have known all along.

Once general vocabulary items are well established, the simple and barely adequate reply 'une glace' 'une limonade', 'des frites', etc. clearly needs extending. 'Et pour vous, Monsieur?' (Display 'coffee' card without verbal support.)

    (Pupil) Un café.
– Dites: Je voudrais un café.
    (Repeat. Chorus if thought necessary.)
– Et pour vous Mademoiselle?
    (One will, of course, expect Je voudrais . . .)
– Et vous, Monsieur? Et vous, Mademoiselle?

A courteous 's'il vous plaît Monsieur' can be fed in in the same way if it does not emerge spontaneously.

Variants of the requesting formula 'Je prends, Moi, je prends; . . . pour moi . . .' may also be introduced in the same way.

As previously implied, though the pupils' utterances are communicative in *form* the activity is not in any other sense communicative. The whole thing is closely controlled by the teacher who, for some of the time will not even allow pupils freedom of choice in what they 'order'. At certain points he will control their choices by cueing those items which have been least well learned or present the most difficulty in pronunciation. Earlier, of course, he will have begun with easily recognised items such as *un café* and *une limonade* in order to get the activity going without unnecessary added difficulties. Increasingly, however, he will call on the least able in the class, for he will not wish to leave this phase until he is sure that all are confidently in possession of the basic items required by the following communicative activity. This task ought to be satisfactorily completed in comfortably under 15 minutes. If it is not, too many items or too many complications have been introduced too quickly. Or questions have been distributed inefficiently – for example too many 'easy' questions have been given to able pupils.

The ablest pupils in the group, having been fully involved in the novel opening minutes, may reasonably be expected to be patient as the activity proceeds and the teacher concentrates on those who are slower to learn.

ORAL WORK IN PAIRS AND GROUPS

The various forms of language teaching that have been practised in the past have each had their own characteristic culminating exercise – the activity in which pupils really showed what they had achieved. In the grammar translation approach this was the prose, the famous Exercise 10, *Traduisez en français*, the moment of truth in which pupils had to put together the new grammar and vocabulary learnt by rote on the first page, exemplified in the reading passage, practised in various gap-filling and substitution exercises and so on. In other approaches the culminating activity has comprised the 'exploitation' of dialogues and structures overlearned by mim–mem in the laboratory or from the tape recorder in the classroom, or the writing of a 'composition' based on a text or set of pictures after they have been thoroughly worked over by means of teacher-centred question and answer.

In a communicative approach in which oral production is regarded as being at least as important as the other three language skills, the culminating activity of a lesson or unit of work will often be oral work in groups or pairs. Brief pair work (especially) may also be used at earlier stages as a way of practising a particular structure, function or range of vocabulary items.

Practice of this kind has certain obvious advantages over other forms of oral work used in the past, such as audio-lingual drilling and teacher-centred question-and-answer work. Whereas this latter form of work, when well done, ensured that the language was at least used meaningfully and produced utterances which were either true (e.g. about the pupils themselves or about the classroom situation), or were supposed to be true, when they related to imaginary characters, they were often not strictly communicative, in that the teacher usually already knew the answer to the question asked. It also, probably, did not allow sufficient practice for either fluency or confidence to be achieved. If, as has been suggested earlier, skilful teacher-centred question-and-answer work remains valuable it is at the stage of presenting new material, or dealing with the question of meaning in unfamiliar texts and recordings, rather than for the sake of oral production.

Drill-type practice has the rather different disadvantage that though it may provide for plenty of practice if carried out in the laboratory or in chorus, it concentrates on improving the pupils' performance at a very superficial level. The pupil practises producing the sounds of the language, or producing a particular kind of utterance, but does little that will develop his competence in choosing when or in what circumstances to say the things he is learning to say. He says what he is required to say, simply because he is required to say it. Even in imagination, he is neither taking the initiative nor using the language to perform any genuine linguistic function. Group work and pair work overcome many of these difficulties. There necessarily remains a high degree of artificiality, but at least these activities make it possible to practise saying the sort of thing that pupils may plausibly need to say in a real situation. In particular, pupils have opportunities for practising utterances that initiate interaction such as asking questions, greeting, making requests and so on, that may often be overlooked in more teacher-centred oral work. Pair work and group work also appear to be enjoyed by pupils who, as many traditional teachers were painfully aware, like interacting with each other more than they like paying attention to what the teacher is doing at the front of the class. They are glad to be 'let off the hook' to take responsibility for their own learning rather than be constantly under the teacher's critical eye. The fact that fluency and effective communication are now regarded as more important than detailed accuracy means that teachers no longer need to be hyper-anxious that pupils will acquire 'bad habits' or 'practise mistakes', though these will, in any case be minimised by careful precommunicative work of the kind described earlier.

Though pair and group work are in principle highly appropriate to current language-teaching objectives, they may, like any other teaching method, be designed and carried out well or badly. Not all such work is equally effective and there remains a constant need for self-criticism and self-appraisal on the part of the teacher. To this end, some of the following considerations may usefully be borne in mind.

Integrating pair work and group work

It is less than maximally productive to begin one's lesson with the words 'Right, last week we did the Post Office. This week it's the cobblers. One of you be the shoe-mender, the other takes in some shoes and asks for them to be repaired. Off you go.' Yet precisely this approach 'from cold' appears to be encouraged by certain supposedly communicative textbooks offering situations for 'role-play practice for GCSE'. Even when a list of vocabulary (with English equivalents!) is provided, such an approach is likely to produce little new learning or self-confidence in pupils.

Even at relatively advanced stages in the course where intensive precommunicative work of the kind described earlier no longer seems appropriate, pupils need to hear or see the language they are to employ being used by someone else before they attempt to use it themselves. To an extent they need to possess it already and will benefit from practising at least the more difficult parts in isolation. Pair work and group work or simple role-play may often arise naturally out of other work the class has been doing, such as reading or listening comprehension, or even the presentation of a new structure. Indeed, whatever other piece of work one is doing, it is always worth considering whether a brief piece of pair work or similar activity may not be drawn from it.

If, for example, one has been looking at a menu or listening to a shop or railway station dialogue for purposes of comprehension, five minutes spent ordering from the menu or making similar purchases or enquiries to those made in the dialogue, are obvious and natural developments.

Moving to a more complex example, let us suppose that as an exercise in listening comprehension, one has been working with a recording of an announcement given out on board the cross-Channel ferry. It concerns, let us say, a delay in the time of arrival, the whereabouts of the duty-free shop, cafeteria and passport office, and also tells passengers what to do with the yellow landing tickets they have been given.

In itself, this is a perfectly valid exercise, but it would be a sorry waste to pass on to new material without some such pair-work task as the following: 'You have heard the announcement but due to noise or distortion you have not fully understood it. So check by asking a (French) fellow passenger, e.g. when you are due to arrive, where there is a shop, where one can eat, where passport control is and whether you have to keep the yellow ticket.'

The other partner, so that he too may have an authentic task, may imagine that he is being asked by a *French* person who, for some reason has not heard properly.

The complexity of pair work

Pair work may be of varying degrees of difficulty and complexity. In the early weeks there will be much value in such simple and closely circumscribed exchanges as:

- Bonjour.
- Bonjour.
- Ça va?
- Oui, ça va, et toi?

– Ça va bien aussi.
– Au revoir.
– Au revoir (serrer la main).

Such rituals, which form an important part of our interactive life, occur virtually unchanged, over and over again and any variation from the normal may either give rise to confusion or simply pass unnoticed. This is equally true of many transactional conversations in shops and various enquiry offices and fairly stereotyped practice of this kind is not at all out of place. Such enquiries (prices, times, whereabouts of buildings) may, however, easily be rendered more realistic if the information is available, preferably in tabular or non-verbal form, only to the person answering. A further dimension may be added if the person asking has to do something on the basis of the information he receives. He may, for example, have to mark a position on a plan or map, or decide whether he has enough money to make his intended purchase.

Pair work and group work do not necessarily become more complex as the course advances. Even at relatively early stages fairly complex activities may involve moving seats and furniture, as well as the use of props, cue-cards, information grids and so on. These may need to be carefully prepared, explained and even to some extent rehearsed if chaos and wasted time is not to result.

In a more advanced class, on the other hand, a new structure or verbal formula may be briefly practised without moving seats or taking more than a few seconds' break in the course of other work. At this stage, however, it is also possible to organise linguistically more demanding and open-ended pairwork, such as the following: 'Using knowledge of the locality (or guidebook information) suggest activities for an apparently rather "difficult" French visitor.' The other partner imagines he is in a French home. He has his own reasons for not wanting to go out and has to give courteous excuses for not taking up the suggestions made to him. In the upper forms of the school pupils may, after due preparation (see Ch. 8), discuss genuinely contentious issues of the kind that may serve as essay topics at A level.

Developing open-ended oral work

Despite the undoubted value of some brief, rather stereotyped exchanges we must seek to devise more imaginative open-structured tasks in the middle and later years if our pupils are to become truly competent communicators. To this end it is always appropriate to ask whether, without loss of efficiency or control, our planned activity could not be adapted or extended to make it more flexible or open-ended. The crucial feature is not the complexity of the utterances our pupils are required to produce but the nature of the guidance we give them. Subject to the requirements of good order, bearing in mind the nature of our particular class, it is desirable to give pupils as much freedom and flexibility as possible so that they have the feeling of genuinely doing their own thing, not only phrasing their requests and enquiries in their own way, but also organising their discourse in the way they feel they are best able to handle. One pupil, for example, may greet the man in the 'Objets trouvés' and launch straight into a detailed account of how he lost his suitcase. Another may prefer to greet and be greeted, state that he has lost a suitcase of a certain colour and then wait upon detailed enquiries from the official. Having the freedom to choose one approach rather than another may lead pupils, with the aid of comments from classmates and teacher, to conclude that one approach is more appropriate than the other, but often these things are a matter of temperament and personal preference.

The most restrictive form of guidance is the reading of printed dialogues or the repeating of ones that are recorded, or that have been virtually or actually learned by heart. Doubtless these activities (especially the latter, see Buckby *et al.* 1986: 45) should not be entirely condemned. But if these activities have become a standard part of one's repertoire some review may be in order, for though they may practise the skill of producing certain utterances once given, they provide no practice in deciding either what to say in a certain situation, or even how to say it.

A slightly more flexible device is guided role-play. Typically in this exercise pupils are given fairly precise instructions (in English or the target language) as to what to say, without being told the actual words to be used. The 'guiding' material may take a number of forms. These include various kinds of cue-cards or conversation cards (see, e.g. Slaney 1986) as well as materials in which the two partners are given different sets of instructions in (for example) A and B books (see e.g. Harris and Roselman 1986; Scullard 1986). Closely guided role-play in which the examiner has a script and the candidate a fairly tight set of instructions is widely used in examinations, where it may be felt necessary to prescribe the responses required of the candidate fairly closely. Doubtless this exercise also has some value in a teaching situation though one hopes that, with its emphasis on 'how you say it' rather than 'what you say' it will not become too automatic or stereotyped a part of the language-learning scene, particularly in forms which are little more than disguised translation.

(A) Say hello.
(B) Say hello. Ask what you can do for him/her?

(A) Say 'Is this deckchair free?'
(B) Say no, it is your father's. He is in the process of bathing and is going to come back in ten minutes' time.
(A) Say you are sorry to have disturbed him.

Clearly, more valid learning would result from a rather more open scenario. After studying an example of a similar conversation in a train or a restaurant, for example, or a beach scene in which at least a deck-chair (or the unavailability of free deckchairs) is mentioned, one might discuss how one might go about asking whether a chair was free. Pupils might be asked to suggest the courtesies appropriate to approaching someone with a request, various ways of phrasing the question, and so on. One might also discuss appropriate ways of responding to such an enquiry, such as not being brusque or disagreeable, while indicating clearly and firmly that the chair was not available. Possibly one might actually rehearse the scene, with participants on opposite sides of the room to make sure that everyone has an opportunity to hear and appraise. One may then simply tell the class to practise the scene a couple of times in pairs, taking it in turns to be the enquirer and the person asked. Provided the preparation has been adequate they will find their own way of acting out the scene, and results will be surprisingly varied as between individuals.

Role-play and communication

We have distinguished between fairly restricted role-play and the performance of language tasks in ways that are much more loosely specified, suggesting that the latter may be more desirable, in so far as this can be reconciled with the demands of effective guidance and control. A further important distinction is that between role-playing and genuine communication. Both undoubtedly have their strengths and neither ought to be entirely neglected. Role-play is essential to enable a full range of useful language to be practised within the confines of the classroom but without at least some genuinely communicative use of the language – actually using the language to ask for information one wants, or giving or understanding requests that have to be carried out – confidence in one's ability to do something in the language may not readily be acquired. This is all part of the argument for school exchanges and visits, pen-friends, use of the 'assistant' and so on, not to mention use of the target language for the purposes of classroom business.

Writers have suggested many genuinely communicative activities and many role-play situations may, with a little thought, be adapted to involve a genuine information gap. Games provide opportunities for genuine communication, provided the pupil is prepared to participate to the extent of attempting to compete or win the game. As a variant to the 'shop' role-play, in which the pupil asks whether the shopkeeper has certain items in stock, one may organise a simple game of happy families in which players attempt to collect (say) four items from the one shop. (The items may be quickly drawn by the pupils themselves on halved index cards.)

The key question and response:

– Est-ce que vous avez . . .?
– Oui j'ai . . . Non, je n'ai pas . . .

occur in both the role-play and the game. The key linguistic elements in many role-play (and, of course authentic) situations may be embodied in games or puzzles of various kinds: 'Madame Legros est sortie avec 150 francs. Elle a acheté trois objets et elle est rentrée avec 38,20 francs. Qu'est-ce qu'elle a acheté?' Pupils are divided into groups only one of whom has the pictures of the various possible purchases marked with prices. The others will need to ask 'Quel est le prix de' . . .? several times before they discover three totalling exactly 110,80 francs.

The seeking and giving of personal information may be practised with cue-cards giving information about imaginary characters, cr pupils may make genuine enquiries of each other. They do not always know each other as well as we think. Narrative ('Saying what you did') may be practised using picture stories, the page from the policeman's notebook or whatever. But equally pupils may cross-question each other (provided they are prepared with appropriate questions and appropriate vocabulary) about how they spent the previous evening or weekend, and then pass the information on to third parties, who may be not a little interested.

Supervising and extending pair and group work

Pair work and group work is not only a means of practising what is known already. It also provides opportunities, both for discreet monitoring of progress and for further teaching. The teacher's first concern in setting his class going on group work must necessarily be to prevent civil disorder and sort out any misunderstandings about what is to be done. Once a good working relationship has been established, however, he is free to intervene in the work of individual pairs or groups, supporting or correcting where necessary, and also suggesting developments and variations to particular groups whose work is going especially well.

The composition of pairs and groups

Something should perhaps be said about how one's groups ought to be composed. Should pupils be allowed to select their own groups on a simple friendship basis, or should the teacher positively intervene to compose groups according to some particular principle such as homogeneity or deliberate mixing (according to, e.g. gender, social class, personality, race or ability)? It is difficult to give any general answer to this question except to say that the teacher should give it some thought from time to time and not simply continue existing practice without reflection. A good principle might seem to be that we should not attempt to control the way pupils want to learn unless there appears to be some clear advantage in doing so. It is a reasonable presumption that pupils will work better and with less inhibitions with classmates they enjoy working with. One might also follow the unfussy and non-invidious principle of having pupils work with those they happen to be sitting nearest to.

Often, however, there may be some positive advantage in intervening. There is no reason why two perfect pests should be allowed to egg each other on to increasingly horrendous atrocities when they can easily be separated. It is also undesirable for the class to degenerate into mutually hostile cliques. Sometimes groups of taciturn boys and giggling girls may be integrated with stimulation and advantage to both. One ought, also no doubt, to strike a sensitive balance between respecting the wishes of an ethnic minority group to stay together and the desirability of integrating them with others. Sometimes, too, a conscious effort may enable one to find a sympathetic 'home' for two or three isolates instead of just leaving them to make do with each other's uninspiring company, *faute de mieux*.

REVIEW AND ENHANCEMENT

1. Consider a first- or second-form unit that you will begin work on shortly.
   (a) Identify the social situation or context to which the new language to be introduced belongs. Consider how familiar this situation will be to your pupils.
   (b) Discuss the situation with your class, as far as possible allowing them to express their perception of it and its linguistic requirements.
   (c) Record the above discussion. Attempt to quantify teacher and pupil inputs. Repeat this process in respect of two or three subsequent units with a view to increasing the quality and quantity of pupil contributions.

2. Identify the next occasion on which you will need to present a substantial piece of new language.
   (a) Identify words and expressions upon which the success of later, less closely controlled work will depend.
   (b) Referring, if necessary to pp 57–62 above, devise ways of presenting these which minimise the use of English. Produce or identify any visuals, texts or other materials that will be required for this purpose.
   (c) With the aid of a recording, assess whether you have ensured adequate mastery before passing on. Identify checking procedures used and name the pupils to whom they were applied. Consider whether satisfactory responses from these pupils constitute sufficient reason for believing that the material was mastered by the class as a whole.
3. Identify a piece of material not primarily intended for practice in oral production (e.g. tape, text, list or public notice).
   (a) Identify one or two linguistic items contained in it, or suggested by it, which merit being brought into active use. Devise appropriate brief pair-work activity.
4. Select a group-work activity suggested by your course, or devise a group-work activity of your own for use with a unit to be studied in the near future.
   (a) Develop or extend the activity for use by one or two abler groups. Present the original activity to the class. Transfer abler groups to the extended activity. After a short time consider whether the whole class might not now attempt the extended activity.
   (b) Identify a piece of language connected with the current topic but not suggested by the course-book. Plan in detail an appropriate pair- or group-work activity to practise it. Discuss the situation to which the language belongs and present any essential words or expressions.
   (c) Ask the class to practise the new piece of language giving an absolute minimum of guidance on the structure of the dialogue. Do not allow pupils to compose a written script. Allow one or two groups to perform their impromptu dialogue for comment and appreciation.
   (d) Select two or three role-play activities from your course or elsewhere. Devise ways of incorporating their linguistic objectives into games or information-gap activities.

FURTHER READING

Littlewood W 1981 *Communicative Language Teaching*. Cambridge University Press, Cambridge

Morgan G. 1987 'Exploiting the natives – making use of native speakers in the classroom', *British Journal of Language Teaching*, **25** (2), 73–8.
Pattison P 1987 *Developing Communication Skills*. Cambridge University Press, Cambridge
Slaney N 1986 'Conversations libres: beyond the conversation card', *British Journal of Language Teaching* **24** (2), 98–103

CHAPTER 5

Writing

Currently it is possible to gain a GCSE Grade E or below in a foreign language without taking a test in writing at all. It also appears that the writing test will be absent from some or all Advanced Supplementary (A/S)-level examinations. For the majority of GCSE candidates, however, the requirement is that they should be able to communicate in the written language. The various examination bodies have helpfully provided a degree of further precision by specifying the sort of task that candidates will be called upon to perform. The NEA, for example (NEA 1986: 6), specifies that candidates taking the basic level test must be able to convey elementary information to and elicit information from both strangers and friends. At the higher level they are required to elicit and convey information, attitudes and opinions in a wider range of situations in response to either written or visual stimuli: the task to be performed by candidates is required to be authentic and precis, dictation and translation are ruled out as possible testing devices. In effect, basic level candidates are required to write brief informal notes or postcards, fill in forms or write simple, closely guided letters of approximately 30–60 words. Higher level candidates write longer letters, narratives or descriptions, of approximately 100 words, of a kind that they might plausibly wish or be required to produce in reality.

The changed status of writing in new language syllabuses has produced a number of problems and dilemmas for language teachers and it must be said that, in both theoretical and practical terms, the situation with regard to the teaching of writing is probably less satisfactory than in relation to the other three language skills.

PUPILS NOT TAKING THE WRITING TEST

The first, and probably the most easily resolved of these dilemmas concerns those pupils who will not take the writing test in the GCSE. Some teachers, and certainly some pupils, might be inclined to ask why, if they are not to attempt the writing test in the examination, they should spend any time writing the language at all or why they should give themselves any trouble attempting to do so correctly.

It is not, at this stage, clear how many pupils are likely to take the non-writing option in the examination, but for a number of reasons one might expect and hope that the number will be relatively small. Even if the number is significant, however, it is unlikely and undesirable that, except perhaps in the extreme case of those suffering from dyslexia or who for some reason have difficulty in forming their letters, they should follow a course in which writing plays no part. It would be an extreme assumption that such pupils will hear, read or have occasion to speak the language but will never, under any circumstances, want to write a word of it down. Possibly there are people who fall into this category, but it is unlikely that we shall be able to predict precisely who they are when they begin their course.

In discussing the teaching of any subject it is often helpful to distinguish between course objectives which may be reflected in examination tests, and those teaching procedures which are the means to their achievement but may not always closely resemble them. For some pupils it may be a desirable examination strategy to economise on revision time by not undertaking last-minute preparation for the writing test. This, however, does not mean that being able to write a few words in the language is not a desirable course objective for them. Far less does it mean that writing should not be used as a learning activity. Most pupils will write the foreign language for two reasons. Firstly, for most of them, to be able to communicate in writing is a full course objective. They write to practise the communication skills, writing informal messages, letters, reports, etc. which it is supposed they may wish to write at some point in the future. But they also write as a learning process. They may write down short lists of words, dialogues, examples of structures or ways of saying things as a means of clarification and reinforcement for later revision. Often, there will be no obvious hard-and-fast distinction between the two kinds of writing. A note asking someone to buy a list of shopping is practice of the communicative writing skill, but also serves to consolidate and record the words in question. Likewise, a letter recounting the events of one's summer holiday may consolidate and record the use of the perfect tense, which may lead to greater ease and fluency in its use in oral work. It is no doubt necessary to preserve some kind of balance between the time spent on the various skills. There is, however, no more pernicious misunderstanding than to suppose that minutes spent on one skill are just so many minutes taken away from progress in the other three. Just as oral practice and discussion may greatly improve the accuracy and coherence of what one writes, so writing may have a beneficial effect on one's oral production.

It may also be a valid way of assessing one's reading or listening comprehension if, for example, the class is asked to write down certain information gained from scanning a passage or listening to a recorded dialogue. There is, therefore, no reason why those who, at the end of the day, do not take the writing test should feel aggrieved at having spent time writing the language in class or for homework.

In a mixed-ability class it is often necessary and certainly possible to differentiate between the level of tasks undertaken by different groups of pupils. Pedagogic and organisational problems would nevertheless arise if there were some pupils present in the class who did no writing. To segregate non-writers into a class of their own at an early stage would be to create a sink stream of pupils expected to gain a Grade E or below. Equally, one may be apprehensive about the psychological effect of defining a pupil as a non-writer with a ceiling of Grade E shortly before the examination. For this reason it seems likely that, except for the case of pupils with particular or severe difficulties, many departments will wish to maintain writing activities right up to and into the examination.

The tendency of substantial numbers of less able pupils to take the non-writing option would also have certain wider implications. The absence or diminished representation of such pupils in the writing examination would inevitably lead to the setting of writing tests which did not cater for the least able pupils and did not allow them to achieve even a minimally satisfactory performance. This in turn would accentuate the tendency of such pupils not to be entered, eventually producing a substantial and recognisable category of non-writers in the foreign language. This would no doubt be followed by efforts to identify such pupils as early as possible in order not to 'waste time' in teaching them to write. Such a move would militate against organisational flexibility and mixed-ability teaching over the full range, and become a convenient shibboleth for labelling an educational underclass of significant proportions.

CREATING OPPORTUNITIES FOR WRITTEN WORK

Little useful guidance regarding the teaching of the written language is to be found in the modern language teaching literature. Woods (1986) is perhaps an honourable exception, but the relevant sections in SEC (1986), DES (1987a) and Partington and Luker (1984) are brief and perfunctory. Benefit may be derived from some works on the teaching of English as a foreign language, such as Abbott and Wingard (1981: 139–70) and Broughton (1978: 116–12).

More troubling is the relative lack of writing activities and exercises in many of the best and most recently published courses. This is in marked contrast to the position with regard to the other three skills. Books on communicative language teaching, as well as modern courses themselves, are full of ingenious, stimulating and highly practical suggestions for group work and pair work and other forms of authentic speaking practice. Most courses also provide a good if perhaps still not entirely adequate supply of material and suggested tasks for reading and listening comprehension. Writing is decidely less well provided for. It would not be fair to desribe as entirely typical Gilogley's *Standard French* (Gilogley 1987) of which the volume on the reading and writing tests devotes 114 pages to reading and four to writing. Few courses, however, suggest as much as one writing activity per unit, and in most the reference to writing is decidely sporadic. *Deutsch Heute* (Sidwell and Capoore 1984/85) which retains a number of traditional features is slightly more generous but is an academically demanding course, and many of its writing activities are of a traditional gap-filling and sentence-completion kind, rather than authentically communicative.

No doubt this imbalance springs partly from a natural desire among modern linguists to cast off the image of modern languages as a mainly written subject and a felt need to provide classroom teachers with viable and practical materials and activities with which to practise the speaking and comprehension skills. Some course-book writers may even have felt that most teachers were, in any case, only too prone to have their pupils writing and needed no encouragement to continue to do so.

In fact, however, the problem may be somewhat more deep-seated than any such temporary pendulum swing away from writing. The fact is that the range of occasions upon which one authentically communicates with speakers of foreign language in writing is relatively limited. One may need to understand a good deal over a range of topics in both speech and writing. Most of one's information and other needs, however, are met through the medium of speech. One cannot write postcards for ever and the variety of notes one can leave for one's French visitor is fairly limited. Many pen-friendships fizzle out after the initial exchange of personal information and the range of written enquiries that even terribly fussy, middle-class persons can make of hotel-keepers, tourist information centres and lost property offices is not extensive.

Many language teachers express anxiety about the possible repetitiveness of examination questions after the novelty of the first few years has worn off. If there is a shortage of varied and authentic tasks for an annual examination it is perhaps small wonder that they are spread rather thinly over the five-year course! Few course-writers will wish to be thought repetitive or tedious, especially in pursuit of the traditional and rather under-valued skill of writing.

The relatively limited range of occasions upon which one needs to write in the foreign language may seem to justify reducing the importance given to the writing test in the examination, and even encouraging the non-writing option by allowing those who take it to achieve a fuller range of grades. This, however, does not seem a desirable policy. Though the variety of authentic tasks upon which to practise the writing skill may be limited, occasions may nevertheless arise, however infrequently, in which the ability to communicate intelligently or, indeed, fairly literately in writing is fairly important or even essential. This is bound to be increasingly the case as trade, travel and other contacts across national frontiers become easier and more frequent.

Even in the mother tongue we do not use writing for the purposes of communication very often, unless we happen to work in some clerical, managerial or professional occupation. But if we are able to communicate in writing with friends and relatives, commercial organisations or officialdom, this is not because we have intensively practised writing communications of this limited kind during our youth, but because of the whole range of writing activities, language puzzles and games, narratives, imaginative and descriptive pieces and many other kinds of writing under-taken during our schooldays. Of course, we should not know how to go about composing either personal or business letters if we had not seen examples of such communications written by others. No doubt, too, we improve with practice. But much of the linguistic competence involved in producing them is acquired in the course of other linguistic activities.

Perhaps, therefore, we should not be too restrictive in our choice of writing activities in the course of the learning process, even though communication skill remains the ultimate objective and must be tested by writing tasks as closely as possible resembling real-life communication in the examination. Even though we may not wish to entirely rule out the writing activities that do not resemble authentic communication, however, it still remains desirable to make as much use of such activities or material as is practicable and consistent with a reasonable degree of variety and interest. Whatever view teachers take of the range of acceptable writing activities, they will almost certainly find it necessary to supplement from their own imaginative resources, those suggested by whatever coursebook they are using.

It is a feature of writing as an activity, in the mother tongue as well as in the foreign language, that it is experienced as a somewhat daunting and inhibiting task if it is not practised regularly. It is not necessary, as some traditional teachers used to claim, that every lesson should end with a period of writing. This would be too rigid. But writing does need to receive its regular portion of lesson and homework time and this has to be deliberately planned for if it is not to be neglected. A change of activity from the boisterousness and stresses of group work or other kinds of oral work to the orderly intensity of individual writing will be welcomed by many pupils, as well as by teachers.

THE VARIETY OF WRITING ACTIVITIES

Often the period of writing will be brief, amounting to no more than copying down new material for record purposes. Depending on the ability of the group, copy-writing, especially in the early stages, is a perfectly valid learning activity. Between copy-writing and writing of a freer, more individual kind, there are a number of transitional activities which are more demanding and more motivating than simple copying, but do not require the pupils to produce a great deal of the foreign language for themselves.

These may include cloze exercises in which certain key words are omitted from a passage and have to be inserted, possibly from a list provided. In a more elementary version, some of the letters of the missing words may be provided as additional clues. Rearranging jumbled sentences or jumbled words or linking the jumbled halves of sentences also appears to be quite enjoyed by younger pupils. In a slightly more advanced version, pupils re-arrange sentences given in random order to produce a letter or similar communication.

Sentence-building from a variety of given elements (as below) is also a useful variant on straighforward copy-writing:

Peux-tu aller	à la boulangerie	m'acheter	un kilo	de beurre
	à la crémerie		un demi-kilo	de pain
	à l'épicerie		un paquet	d'oranges
	à la fruiterie		six tranches	de jambon
			une boite	d'œufs
				de fromage

If the sentences to be written can be such as might form part of a real-life written communication, so much the better. Such activities are also exercises in reading comprehension and are often given as such. It is, however, important to decide clearly the purpose for which an activity is being used. Where such activities are used to develop comprehension they may be completed by simply marking a worksheet. Where the purpose is to develop writing skill, and serve as a transition between copy-writing and free writing the teacher will frequently require the sentences or passages in question to be copied out neatly, carefully and in full.

More genuinely communicative but still relatively easily managed writing acivities include those in which pupils, in pairs, take turns in asking and answering questions about themselves in writing, or cooperate in composing descriptions of other members of the class for guessing or 'police identification' purposes. Here the activity is not really authentic in that it does not correspond to any obvious 'real-life' situation, but is genuinely communicative in the sense that the message has to meet the standard of intelligibility if the activity is to work.

Moving towards the production of more authentic messages, it is always desirable when some other substantial piece of work to develop one of the other skills is being undertaken, to consider whether a writing task cannot be based upon it. In many cases this possibility will be obvious, and will sometimes be suggested by the course-book. Units on the giving and eliciting of personal information often include a hotel 'fiche' to complete, or suggest the listing of details to send to a pen-friend organisation. This may be followed by an actual letter to the imaginary pen-friend. Units on the home and family settings and topics may reasonably give rise to similar letters, as may those units aimed at developing the 'saying what you did' function as the work here naturally centres on saying what one has done at the weekend, or during the holidays, or narrating some newsworthy incident or event that one has witnessed or taken part in. Written communications also arise fairly naturally out of the function of making arrangements to meet or visit someone and even the giving of directions. Slightly more ingenuity may suggest a postcard or letter following a meal out (unit on ordering a meal, etc.), a clothes-shopping expedition or a journey. Conceivably one may need to leave a note of a telephone call on a range of topics for one's foreign hosts, or ask one's visitors to pop down to the shop for a list of groceries. If one is at all literal minded about the notion of authentic communication tasks one may feel that some difficulty is involved in drawing writing activities from work on such topics as visits to the doctor, the bank or the filling-station. Nevertheless, one may need to send or leave notes to explain that one is ill and cannot keep an appointment, or is temporarily absent when one's friends arrive because one has had to go out to the bank or filling-station before they close.

Many pupils may still have parents, or at least grandparents, who may not be entirely fluent in the language and would therefore find it helpful to have something written down to give to the doctor or the bank clerk. Stretching the imagination rather more, some pupils might be willing to envisage working for French private detective agencies who, for whatever reason, may require notes to be made on the requirements of customers and others whose transactions have constituted an earlier aural comprehension exercise.

It may be felt that if any degree of ingenuity is required to devise written activities in relation to a particular topic, that is simply an indication that use of the written medium is unlikely to be required in that context, and that time should therefore not be wasted practising its use. This, however, is a rather mean-spirited interpretation of the principle of utility. We cannot know for certain who will be required to write what in the future and it would be illiberal and counter-productive to limit our pupils to practising precisely those transactions which there is a good chance they will have to perform in future. The competence and flexibility to meet an unpredictable range of requirements is the aim rather than inculcating a finite list of written performances to meet a range of predictable situations.

NOT EXAGGERATING THE IMPORTANCE OF THE WRITING SKILL

Writing activities necessarily follow rather than precede work on the other skills, for there is little benefit in having pupils write down language with which they are not already familiar from other contexts. Writing activities arising out of other work will therefore tend to come at the end of a unit or lesson, or be given for homework for which the other work done on the material forms part of the preparation. There is therefore some danger that the writing activity will come to be seen as the culmination or end-point of the unit or lesson; the activity *for the sake of which* dialogues have been listened to, reading passages read and the use of relevant vocabulary practised orally. There is, perhaps, some risk that in one's anxiety to ensure that the writing exercise is well prepared, so that mistakes and incoherences are minimised, one will concentrate on those linguistic items that will be particularly useful when it comes to writing and even tend to limit one's oral practice to what is required for the written exercise to be adequately done. For this reason it is essential that most of one's writing activities should be brief and frequent, often no more than a quick finishing off of some more extended and ambitious activity to practise one of the other three skills.

CORRECTING PUPILS' WRITTEN WORK

For many teachers the correction of pupils' work will present more of a dilemma in relation to writing than to oral work. In assessing oral work, traditional teachers have been fairly tolerant of errors of tense, gender, case and so on, possibly on the grounds that these are only 'slips' arising from the fact that the pupil does not have the time to 'think things through'. In writing, on the other hand, particular sentences or questions have often been specifically set to test precise knowledge of such points. Errors in writing have always been marked and almost always penalised. For many teachers, to leave a 'mistake' unmarked will seem like positive dereliction of duty. There is here a perfectly genuine dilemma which is not to be swept aside by saying that 'communication is all that matters'. As was suggested in Chapter 1 its solution may to some extent lie in distinguishing clearly for oneself and for one's pupils, between those shortcomings in a piece of writing that are of major importance because they actually prevent communication from taking place, and those which are of less significance. The fact remains, however, that these latter are still best put right, for although they do not in themselves make understanding impossible, they may nevertheless distract the reader or result in the message being given less serious attention than might otherwise have been the case. In this connection it should be said that the criteria for assessment of at least one board seem to suggest at one point that, at the higher level, marks may be gained or lost for accuracy alone, even when this does not actually affect communication (NEA 1986: 139). Elsewhere, however, it appears that accuracy is only to be assessed in so far as it helps or impedes communication.

Placing communication above grammatical correctness enables many pupils to achieve something of obvious value in the language who would not have been able to do so in response to more traditional tests. It does not of itself, however, necessarily imply any decline in standards and may actually be the more rigorous criterion. Supposing that pupils are told to write to a certain hotel asking four questions, including whether there is a supermarket within walking distance. Those who cannot produce the word for a supermarket, or an intelligible circumlocution will lose a substantial proportion of the marks allotted, whereas on a traditional basis of one mark off per mistake and two for gross grammatical errors he might still finish up with 19 out 20, despite the fact that the word for a supermarket has to be a key word in any foreign visitor's vocabulary.

In addition to knowing all the right words we may expect our pupils in a communicative examination to show qualities of courtesy, order and other requirements of composition. He may be expected to write in an appropriate style and tone and be especially senstive to the need to avoid ambiguity or irrelevance. Even where a sentence is comprehensible and grammatically correct it is possible to ask whether it could not have been better put to avoid possible misunderstanding, or an apearance of abruptness or naivety that might result in a less sympathetic or less helpful reply. With our best pupils it is possible to aim for extremely high standards on this score. We are here pursuing no banal or purely utilitarian aim, but the classical ideals of economy, clarity and consideration for the reader and his point of view.

In considering what attitude we should take to grammatical and orthographical errors which do not in themselves affect communication, it is necessary to distinguish fairly clearly between the requirements of assessment and those of teaching. It is certain that some errors which under a traditional regime would have been considered 'gross' and heavily penalised would not make the slightest difference to the communcation of the message and, on even a moderately sympathetic native reader, would not even make any kind of bad impression or cause the message to be taken less than seriously. These include such things as the omission on the agreement of the past participle in 'combien de villes avez-vous visitées?' omission of the 'e' in 'nous partageons' or of the 'n' in 'die grossen Häuser'. Indeed, some boards clearly indicate that a knowledge of these or similar points is not required.

For teaching purposes, however, the situation is slightly less simple, given that one is concerned not just with judging and appraising the present piece of work but also with guiding the pupil's performance in the future. Something incorrectly written may not affect the present communication, but if attention is not drawn to it, it may be taken as a model for future writing where it may prove misleading or distracting. Some attention may also be due to the educational aim of encouraging careful and accurate writing (see Aim 7 – 'promoting other education skills') provided this is not destructive of pupil's ability and readiness to communicate confidently in the language. Not every mistake is to be treated with the same degree of seriousness, and we shall not necessarily give the same error the same treatment when it is made by different pupils. For some, to have written anything meaningful at all is already an achievement and we shall naturally be pleased that they have made the effort and achieved so much. With others we can afford to be more demanding. We require not a rule of thumb as to what should or should not be corrected, but guidelines for the exercise of principled flexibility and a clear conception of what we aim to achieve when we comment on a pupil's work.

The following example may help to illustrate these remarks. After suitable preparation, a group of fourth-year pupils is encouraged to attempt a writing task presented in the following terms:

You are staying at the Hôtel de la Place Jeanne d'Arc in Rouen for a fortnight. You called to see a French friend who lives in the town on Wednesday but he was out. A couple of days later you decide to let him know you are in town and send him a note to say you will call again the next Monday evening.

One pupil writes the following, which shows a good sense of what needs to be communicated but contains a number of important and some less important linguistic shortcomings: 'Je passe vous voir mercredi. Vous n'est pas là. Je suis dans Rouen cinquante jours. Je staying à l Hotel de la Place Jeanne d'Arc. Je vais jeudi prochaine.'

Some things clearly need correction on the communicative criterion. *Cinquante* is clearly a mistake for *quinze* and could certainly result in the French person coming to the hotel and finding that his English friend had left long ago. In any case, numbers will often be vital to communication and there really can be no two ways about the importance of getting them right.

'Staying' must be regarded as unintelligible, for though the native speaker is allowed to be sympathetic, he must not be supposed to have either exceptional powers of deduction, or any knowledge of English. *Suis*, or *demeure*, both of which will doubtless be known to the pupil, will need to be suggested.

From the point of view of intelligibility there are two further major points to be dealt with – namely the ambiguities of the first and last sentences. *Je passe* must be corrected because it is not absolutely clear, though it may perhaps be deduced, that it relates to an abortive visit last Wednesday rather than a promised one next Wednesday. It is important that *this* reason for our correction should be clearly communicated rather than that *Je passe* is the 'wrong tense'. In this respect classroom teachers will be aware how commonly the inability to handle past tenses may give rise to ambiguities of this kind in practical communication. This, rather than any more general concern with 'grammar' is a reason for insisting on their being used correctly by pupils capable of doing so.

In the last sentence it is not clear whether the writer is leaving Rouen next Thursday, or is promising a further visit. If *pars* is suggested instead of *vais* it must be made clear that it is because it removes this ambiguity rather than simply because it is 'more idiomatic'. These would appear to be the only errors likely to impair communication substantially, and these must therefore receive the main emphasis if we are to gain credibility for our claim to be primarily concerned with communication rather than grammatical accuracy for its own sake.

There remain 'vous n'est pas là' which a traditional marker would probably have pounced upon as the gravest and most palpable error in the passage, plus such minor points as *dans Rouen*, *prochaine* and the circumflex missing from *hôtel*. What one does about the last three will depend not on any hard-and-fast rule of thumb, but upon two countervailing principles. These are:

1. There is no point in making a correction unless learning is likely to result from it. Returning a *'copie ensanglantée'* is demotivating and a plethora of minor corrections may distract attention from those which are of major importance.
2. Against this, however, one does not wish to create the impression that it does not much matter what or how one writes. One owes one's pupils feedback on their performance, and feedback may be necessary if they are to improve. The only grounds for withholding it are that it may be counterproductive, either because it is demotivating or because it distracts attention from more imporant matters.

In the present case I would suggest, albeit tentatively, that for many pupils the most helpful response would be an explicit but relatively light and inconspicuous amendment. This must certainly be done in the case of 'Vous n'est pas là' for though this is unlikely to cause misunderstanding in the present case, systematic failure to operate the full range of tenses or other fundamental structures of the language may severely restrict what the pupil is able to communicate with fluency and precision.

Let this correction be made, however, in the fairly easily comprehensible terms of the distinction between is/was/were rather than such mystifying generalities as 'the imperfect tense' or 'correct persons of the verb'.

So far we have discussed the correction of pupils' written work in a rather detached way as if it had been simply set, done and handed in to be marked. This, no doubt, is how things are sometimes done, especially in the last two years or so of the main school. On receiving work back, pupils will probably give one's amendments and comments a cursory glance, note that they have scored a passing 6 out of 10 and, if one is lucky, carry out some minimal formal corrections. This may be a perfectly acceptable pattern towards the end of the course when copious practice and independent work are important. At earlier stages, however, it is a singularly unproductive way of dealing with written work.

We earlier mentioned the importance of a gentle and controlled transition from copy-writing to writing of a freer and more independent kind. This entails the careful grading of one's writing tasks and, especially in the early stages, careful supervision of pupils' books. The purpose of this is not to submerge oneself beneath an overwhelming burden of marking, but to keep track on how well pupils are coping. For the most part one will have few corrections to make and much of the necessary marking can usually be carried out while pupils are writing in class. The first sign that things are going wrong is a sharp decline in the accuracy, order and appearance of pupils' work. A reduction in the amount of writing given on a particular occasion, the provision of more time, more carefully structured guidance and generally more support, will usually put matters right.

Throughout the majority of the course it is desirable, as far as possible, to pursue a smooth transition from one's first approach to a new writing task to whatever formal version pupils eventually hand in to be marked. The more stages involved in the transition and the more ways the language in question is mulled over, the better. The first stage will normally be the provision of models, often doubling as comprehension work. This will no doubt be accompanied by discussion of the communicative needs of the situation, drawing attention to vocabulary and other linguistic elements essential to this kind of situation. Possibly these will be copied down from the board.

We are now in a position to begin work on the writing task proper. After guidance, dicussion and possibly some collective class efforts, pupils will no doubt attempt their own rough version of particular messages, either individually or in groups. These need to be read back, discussed and amended in an appropriately positive way. Pupils may then be encouraged to amend and develop their own efforts in the light of this discussion, incorporating and making use of each other's ideas wherever this is helpful. Only when this process has been gone through does it make sense for pupils to attempt a full-dress piece of work to be handed in for marking. It is, after all, an extremely ineffective use of the teacher's time to mark and correct something that is less than the best the pupil could have produced with more adequate preparation.

When the pupil's best efforts are finally given in it is important that any remaining shortcomings should be dealt with in such a way that pupils do not feel rebuked or put down for their stupidity but welcome the teacher's comments as helpful suggestions as to how, in future, they might make an even better job of whatever they have been trying to achieve.

REVIEW AND ENHANCEMENT

1. Maintain a record of all writing activities (in best or rough, however brief) undertaken by a particular class over a period of a month.

(a) On the basis of this consider whether sufficiently regular writing practice is being given. (No attempt is here made to suggest how much writing practice should be given. The teacher should, however, be aware of how much is being done and this should reflect conscious policy.)

(b) Review work done 'in best' during the last half-term. Consider whether this constitutes an adequate record of work covered.

(c) If the above reviews reveal insufficient writing being done, revise your lesson plans daily for the next few weeks with a view to adding a brief writing activity wherever possible.

2. Categorise written work done by one class over a given period, e.g. copy-writing and notes, language exercises, independent writing of communicative tasks.

(a) Attempt to quantify the amount of writing falling into each category and consider strategies for increasing the last.

(b) With the above in mind, consider the next unit to be studied by the class. Note any independent writing activities indicated. Identify and develop further independent writing activities arising out of or suggested by other activities or materials contained in the unit.

3. Review the quality of a recent, fairly extensive piece of written work by your class.

(a) Plan a similar piece of work on a new topic, paying particular attention to its preparation with the class. Identify and present the language that pupils will require and ensure that this is noted. Discuss a related model or models in detail. Set the new task to be drafted in rough. Have several pupils' efforts read out, discussed and amended in class. Give adequate class or homework time for writing up, stressing the importance of care and good presentation.

(b) Compare quality with previous piece.

4. Prepare and set an extensive piece of writing (letter, description, account) to third or fourth-year pupils likely to attempt higher-level writing.

(a) Before marking consider your corrections to a similar piece of work marked previously in the light of the following questions.(i) Have you automatically marked out all mistakes? Does the grade awarded reflect the number of these rather than the quality of the pupils' communication?(ii) Where you have indicated (e.g. by heavier marking) that some mistakes are graver than others, is this because of their grammatical significance or because of their interference with communication? (iii) Have you explicitly drawn attention to parts of the message that have not been adequately communicated? Have you required these shortcomings rather than grammatical errors to be put right in any corrections the pupils have done?(iv) Would brief grammatical explanation have been helpful in the case of some frequently occurring or obtrusive errors?

(b) Now mark the new piece of work bearing in mind reflections arising from the questions above.

FURTHER READING

Allen E D and Valette R M 1972 *Classroom Techniques: Foreign Languages and English as a Second Language*. New York Harcourt Brace Jovanovich, pp. 284–324

DES 1987 *Modern Foreign Languages to 16*. London HMSO

Johnson K 1981 *Communication in Writing*. Longman, London

Woods S 1986 'Developing writing skills in the context of GCSE' in M Buckby et al. *Teaching Modern Languages for the GCSE*. British Association for Language Teaching/Modern Language Association, Leeds, pp. 20–8

CHAPTER 6

Questioning

It has long been recognised (see Cohen 1982: 3–5) that questioning is one of the most central and effective of all pedagogic techniques. As a mode of exposition it has a number of important advantages over unbroken teacher monologue. If sensitively handled it has substantial motivational value. Pupils are glad to show what they know and enjoy the sense of having worked out something for themselves. The teacher's response to their answer serves to confirm or disconfirm their own conclusions. Perhaps even more important, however, is the fact that pupils' answers to judiciously framed questions provide teachers with valuable information as to how much the class understands. They are then able to avoid wasting time and boring the class by going in detail over what is already understood or, if they received inaccurate or incomplete replies, they know exactly what teaching has to be done.

The general topic of questioning technique has been discussed by many writers (see Perrott 1982: 55–99). In language teaching, questions have a number of further highly, specific roles to play (McNair 1973; Wringe 1976: 25–35; 1977) both in discovering what pupils understand or can perform already, and in bringing about understanding or providing opportunities for them to practise new language.

A fundamental operation in language teaching is presenting pupils with a new piece of 'text'. For present purposes this somewhat broad term is taken to embrace not only printed and other written materials (e.g. on the overhead projector, blackboard or a hand-out) but also audio and video recordings. This activity may be intended to develop reading or listening comprehension, but it may also be used to present and practise the use of new material which will later be employed communicatively.

If our material has been correctly graded it will not be entirely understood by most of our pupils right away and the task of bringing them to an adequate understanding may sometimes require fairly intensive assistance from the teacher.

In what follows it is assumed that:

1. Pupils should become actively involved in arriving at meanings for themselves, for only thus are comprehension strategies likely to be developed.
2. Use of the mother tongue is to be minimised.

This process of bringing pupils to an understanding of a piece of new material without use of the mother tongue has sometimes been described as 'explication' or 'explaining' the meaning to the class. Such terms are fundamentally misleading (Wringe 1976: 8–9) and remind one of the perfectly valid charge levied against old-fashioned, direct methodists, of attempting to explain the obvious by means of the recondite. Those who literally attempt to explain a text in a foreign language are almost inevitably doomed to failure. They begin by not knowing whether the original text is understood and then cannot be sure whether the explanation is understood either, or simply produces further confusion.

The question 'Avez-vous compris?' not to say 'Avez-vous tout compris?' is unhelpful, for even if we could entirely rely upon our pupils' candour, we do not always know what we do or do not understand. Indeed, we quite properly wish our pupils to develop the habit of filling in the gaps in their understanding with intelligent hypotheses which they confidently accept until they are falsified.

The correct strategy in dealing with meaning, therefore, is not to attempt to explain at all but, having presented the text, to question and probe with the initial intention of finding out how much is understood, and therefore needs no further comment. Further questions may then be used to extend pupils' comprehension in a number of ways. Some will draw attention to key parts of the text which are important for its meaning. Others help the process of understanding by forcing pupils to make intelligent guesses about the meaning of new words or expressions which are confirmed or disconfirmed by the teacher's response. Questioning may also be used to secure the active use of items required for later productive work or draw attention to the cultural content of the material.

These points may, perhaps, best be illustrated by considering the teaching potential of two texts, one at fifth-form level and one to be exploited in greater detail in the second form.

LA PRESSE

The opening page of Stage 5, Unit 11 of Michael Buckby's *Action! Graded French* appears in Fig 6.1 opposite.

A principal objective of the unit is that pupils should be able to discuss French and English newspapers with a French person of their own age, and also read a newspaper article (in either English or French) with a measure of perception and criticism. The main passage falls into three parts. The first raises the question of how many people in France and elsewhere read a news-

11 LA PRESSE

Objectif

Ceux et celles qui s'intéressent à la France et qui veulent apprendre le français feraient bien de s'intéresser aussi à la presse française. Un des meilleurs moyens de bien connaître la France et sa langue, c'est de lire régulièrement un journal français. Et il y en a pour tous les goûts, comme vous le verrez dans cet Objectif.

Quel journal acheter?

En général, on lit moins de journaux en France que dans la plupart des autres pays d'Europe. En effet, la France n'est que le vingtième pays du monde pour le nombre de journaux par habitant. Selon un sondage récent, seulement 45% des Français lisent un quotidien tous les jours, et 23% ne lisent jamais le journal.

Il y a plusieurs quotidiens nationaux, en France. Il y a des journaux sérieux comme *Le Monde* et des journaux populaires, comme *France-Soir*. Dans les journaux sérieux, on trouve moins de photos et davantage d'articles sur la politique et sur les questions internationales. Dans les quotidiens populaires, il y a davantage de bandes dessinées, d'histoires drôles et ce qu'on appelle les «faits divers». *L'Équipe* est un journal entièrement consacré aux informations sportives.

Plusieurs journaux français vous donnent une bonne idée des opinions politiques des gens qui les lisent. *L'Aurore*, par exemple, est un journal très conservateur. *Le Figaro* aussi est un journal de tendance droite. *Libération* est plutôt à gauche et *L'Humanité* est le journal du parti communiste.

Voici des questions qu'un visiteur dans votre pays pourrait vous poser. Pourriez-vous y répondre, pour le pays où vous habitez?

Il y a, à peu près, combien de quotidiens nationaux?
Lesquels d'entre eux sont des journaux sérieux?
Lesquels sont plus populaires?
Quelles sont les plus grandes différences entre les deux?
Y a-t-il des journaux qui ont une tendance politique marquée?
Selon vous, quel est le meilleur journal?
Et lequel est le pire?

Dès que vous aurez préparé vos réponses aux questions ci-dessus, demandez à votre partenaire de jouer le rôle du visiteur français et de vous poser toutes ces questions.

Ensuite imaginez que c'est vous, le visiteur français dans votre pays, et posez des questions similaires sur les revues hebdomadaires et mensuelles qu'on trouve dans votre pays. Votre partenaire essaiera d'y répondre, avec le sourire!

Source: Adapted from M Buckby *Action, Graded French Book S,* Nelson 1985

paper. The second presents the concepts and vocabulary of serious and popular papers and their typical contents. The third presents the notion of political tendency and gives some examples of papers from various parts of the political spectrum. Effective use of this passage entails:

1. Raising the issue of newspaper reading as an activity undertaken by many people, including people of the age of our pupils, and drawing attention to possible differences of practice as between one country and another.
2. Establishing the notion of the different kinds of papers and their contents as outlined in paragraphs two and three (Fig. 6.1), together with vocabulary involved, e.g. *journal sérieux, populaire, bande dessinée, faits divers, article politique, journal de tendance gauche, conservateur, sondage d'opinion,* etc. To this may, perhaps, be added some vocabulary of general relevance not actually present in the text, such as:*hebdomadaire, revue, revue féminine, comique, magazine, journaliste, reporteur*.

Successful communicative work on later parts of the unit depends on these two objectives being achieved. Additionally, there are certain cultural goals to be achieved. That only 45 per cent of French people, less than in many other countries, read a newspaper, as well as the names and characteristics of various well-known French newspapers is significant background information. The fact that newspapers in either Britain or France fall into the various categories mentioned may itself also constitute news for some fifth-formers.

One way of handling this material might be to simply ask the class to read it for themselves and test for gist comprehension by means of a number of 'true or false' questions:

Vrai ou faux?

1. Les Français lisent plus de journaux que les autres Européens.
2. Les bandes dessinées se trouvent uniquement dans les journaux sérieux.
3. L'Aurore est un journal socialiste, etc., etc.

The task of answering these questions would certainly motivate a reasonable fifth-form class to read the passage with some care and would direct attention to the key point in each paragraph. It would also ensure that certain vocabulary was at least noted in passing. Even with these three questions only, confident accurate replies by all members of the class would indicate a good measure of gist comprehension.

Gist comprehension would also be tested less formally by means of oral questioning:

– Alors parlez-moi un peu du texte.
– Les Français, lisent-ils plus de journaux que les Américians, les Allemands?
– Est-ce que tous les Français lisent un journal tous les jours?
– Qu'est-ce qu'on a fait pour savoir cela?
– Quelles espèces de journaux y-a-t-il?
– Si on s'intéresse à la politique française, quel journal va-t-on acheter?
  etc., etc.

Let us suppose, however, that the response to this procedure gives us little reason for confidence or that, for whatever reason, we feel that our class should study this particular piece more intensively, with rather more input from ourselves. If this were the case we might begin by asking a number of quite factual 'focusing' questions, addressing these in the first instance to some of our less linguistically able or attentive pupils. In this way we might draw attention to the title of the text (*La Presse*) and to the visuals. We might ask what is being sold at the newspaper stand and in what country, the (only partly legible) names of some of the papers, and so on. We might ask what the girl in the picture is doing. If we can also get them to tell us that she is about 16 (the same age as themselves) appears intelligent, pleasant and so on, so much the better.

– Alors, dans ce chapitre, il s'agit de quoi, croyez-vous?

Hopefully, replies to this question will confirm that the task of focusing is accomplished. We are now in a position to address the text. In a younger form, bearing in mind that we are concerned with the precommunicative stage of presentation rather than immediately with communication itself, we might read the text, or the first paragraph of the text, aloud to the class. In the fifth year we may prefer to credit the class with being able to read the text silently, even though the whole meaning may not be immediately clear.

This done we may need briefly to refocus the class's attention.

– Alors, de quoi s'agit-il ici?
(Des journaux.)
– Oui, mais où? En quel pays?
– D'accord. Alors maintenant *regardez le premier paragraphe*, etc.

If oral presentation and textwork fail to achieve the expected response it is often for lack of this kind of attention management.

Frequently, pupils simply do not know where to look in order to make sense of the teacher's questions.

In the first paragraph the only vocabulary likely to prove a problem is *sondage, quotidien* and perhaps *habitant*. The meaning of the second sentence, however, may seem a trifle abstruse. By starting with the general sense of the paragraph, however, we may find that our class will have made and confirmed for themselves reasonable hypotheses on all these points.

– Est-ce que tous les Français lisent un journal tous les jours?
– Combien (quel pourcentage) des Français lisent un journal tous les jours?
– Et les autres 22%?
– Comment est-ce qu'on sait cela?
– Comment est-ce qu'on sait combien de gens lisent un journal,
– combien de femmes aiment les hommes chauves, voteront conservateur, etc? Alors, pour savoir cela on fait . . . ?

At this point someone is almost bound to volunteer 'On fait un sondage'. The term 'sondage d'opinion', though not strictly accurate here, might have the advantage of being more readily understood, if that were felt to be necessary.

Anxious teachers, wishing to be assured of complete comprehension may wish to ask a rather slow member of the class:

– Alors, un sondage, c'est quoi en anglais? Hopefully, however, most will not feel it necessary to do so.

An important point to note is that there has been no attempt to 'explain' the meaning of *sondage*. It has been arrived at by bringing pupils to want to use it in an appropriate situation.

– Est-ce qu'il y a des pays où les gens lisent plus de journaux que les Français?
– Combien?

A confident 'dix-neuf' from a pupil chosen at random would indicate comprehension of the aforementioned second sentence. Its absence might lead one to ask pupils where the most newspapers are probably read. And then where? And then?

One might begin to build up a list

1. L'Amérique.
2. L'Angleterre.
3. . . . Non, ce n'est pas la France.
   En effet, la France, c'est le numéro . . . ?

The word *quotidien* will probably be understood by now, but is worth drawing attention to.

– Regardez ce mot 'quotidien'.
– Alors, qui peut me donner le nom d'un journal quotidien anglais?

The *Daily Mirror* or the *Sun* will indicate comprehension. Should someone volunteer the *News of the World*, this will provide an opportunity to ask whether the paper in question is 'un quotidien' or 'un hebdomadaire' i.e. this double question enables a new word to be 'fed in' unobtrusively.

With prompting we could, of course, obtain the reply that 'un quotidien' is 'un journal qui paraît tous les jours', that 'un hebdomadaire paraît une fois par semaine' and so on. There is no great harm in this, provided confirming examples are also sought. The temptation to avoid, however, is for the *teacher* to attempt to explain that 'Un quotidien, c'est un journal qui paraît tous les jours' and suppose that comprehension was thereby assured.

Similar procedures may be used with the subsequent paragraphs, remembering that it is important to establish the concepts of the serious and popular press. If pupils can volunteer appropriate English examples this may be taken to indicate that the concept is grasped and that no specific explanation is required.

– Les histoires de Mickey Mouse, de Tintin, d'Astérix, c'est quoi? Regardez le texte, deuxième paragraphe vers la fin, vous trouverez l'expression.
– Et l'histoire d'un homme qui mord un chien? C'est quoi?
– Alors, maintenant, vous êtes à Paris et vous voulez lire le rapport d'un match de Rugby France–Angleterre. Vous achetez quel journal français?
– Et si on veut lire . . .?

The notion of political bias in newspapers may be relatively unknown to some pupils, but others may be able to furnish examples of an English paper 'qui favorise le parti conservateur/ socialiste (travailliste)', etc.

Possibly at this point it might be useful to return to the photo of the newspaper stand, with its scarcely legible titles and ask pupils to identify the various papers on display, and say something about each of them.

If part of the purpose of this activity is to enable pupils to discuss aspects of the press with an imaginary French visitor, certain not too difficult pieces of vocabulary will need to be actively mastered by the whole class. Before leaving this part of the work, therefore, we shall go to some trouble to ensure and check that, e.g. 'un quotidien', or 'de tendance conservatrice' can be produced by some of the less able members of the class in response to 'testing' questions which do not contain them.

INTENSIVE WORK ON A SECOND-YEAR TEXT

At the relatively advanced stage considered in the previous section it may be assumed that pupils have a good deal of language at their disposal and, though some teacher-centred question and answer work may be used to ensure that both content and certain linguistic details are noted, the process need not be either complex or intensive. At earlier stages, however, with pupils who are less able to take responsibility for their own learning, teachers may feel the need for some reliable oral techniques not depending on use of the mother tongue both for establishing whether meaning is understood and for remedying the situation when it is not.

Let us suppose that we have recently taken over a somewhat mixed and not very able group of second-formers part way through the year. Though not positively ill-disposed they have, for whatever reason under their previous teacher, become somewhat disaffected. They have little confidence in their ability to understand anything of which they have not explicitly been told the meaning and are reluctant to speak at all. Clearly our first task is to establish a good, supportive relationship, encourage them to respond and reward them with approval for doing so.

We should like to get them to be able to work in pairs, telling each other some of the things they do at the weekend. Sports are reasonably well established in the school but not all participate. Some pupils, no doubt, stay at home, help their parents, go round to see friends, go into town, watch matches on television and so on. As a starting-point we have the following text with, perhaps an appropriate illustration.

Voilà Pauline. Elle est tout près de l'arrêt d'autobus. Elle tient sa raquette de tennis. Ses vêtements de sport (jupe blanche, chemisier, chaussettes, chaussures, etc.) sont dans son sac. Tous les samedis d'été elle va jouer au tennis pour l'équipe de son école. Le terrain des sports est à trois kilomètres de chez elle. Il est maintenant une heure 25. L'autobus va arriver dans cinq minutes.

Our immediate aim is to have the text fully understood and key vocabulary capable of being actively produced. We also eventually wish to introduce a certain amount of parallel vocabulary, for example in addition to 'Elle/je joue au tennis', we wish to introduce 'Je joue au football/Rugby/ping-pong/hockey, je reste à la maison/je vais en ville/j'aide ma mère/je travaille dans le magasin de mes parents', etc. Along with 'Elle prend/je prends l'autobus' we also wish to teach 'Je vais à pied/en vélo/dans la voiture de mon père' and so on.

When text and illustration are closely linked, as in the present imaginary case, it is often desirable, having once read through the text, to switch attention to the illustration allowing pupils to refer to the text as a source of information and relevant vocabulary. The aim is, after all, to talk meaningfully about persons, things and events, rather than simply lift pieces from the text. Even when there is no illustration it is desirable to liberate pupils from the text by concentrating on its subject-matter rather than working through the sentences that compose it in the order in which they occur. Gradually, by repeatedly scanning the text for the information and language they need to make their contribution to the work of the class, pupils will come to an understanding of most of it.

– Regardez la jeune fille (focusing utterance).

This, like all our utterances, is an exercise in aural comprehension. We should therefore avoid such actions as holding up the book, pointing at the picture and so on if we think there is a fair chance we shall be understood. Our aim is to teach French rather than sign language. Although paralinguistic communication is often helpful in getting something understood on the first few occasions, it is obviously essential to wean pupils off any such dependence as soon as possible.

We must nevertheless check that our instruction has been understood by noting whether or not our pupils are looking at the right part of the page.

– Michael, tu regardes la jeune fille?

We may perhaps point for Michael's sake. In his case it may be necessary.

– Alors, c'est qui, la jeune fille?

No answer.

Hopefully, there normally would be an answer, but let us take the most pessimistic view in order to explore the extent of the resources available to the teacher who wants to maximise his use of the target language rather than revert to the mother tongue. 'Alors, c'est qui? C'est Sharon? C'est Jacqueline? C'est Katie? (Girls in the class.) 'C'est Simone? Oui ou non?' Yes/no questions are often one's salvation in a turgid situation, the more so given that it is always possible, as a very last resort, to cheat by signalling the desired answer by nodding or shaking the head. 'C'est Simone? (Shake, shake.) Non, c'est Margaret? Non, c'est Liz? C'est Jean? C'est Pauline?' (We shall get 'non'.) Ce n'est pas Pauline? (Nod, nod.) Si c'est Pauline. C'est qui? C'est qui? C'est qui? (To a variety of different members of the class.)

This is our breakthrough, so let us give as many of them as possible the chance to say it. 'D'accord, c'est Pauline. Alors, dites-moi quelque chose sur Pauline.'

This will almost certainly be a conversation stopper. But we ought to try to use this kind of very open-ended question as much as we can. This kind of stimulus encourages pupils to pick out whatever seems to be of particular interest to them, or, in a text that is largely mystifying, whatever they can understand, however general or fragmentary that may be. Questions like 'De quoi s'agit-il ici?' 'Que pensez-vous du jeune homme qui parle?' are similarly open-ended questions. If we can get pupils to respond we are half-way to the point where they actually volunteer comment spontaneously. An inviting 'Alors?' with an encouraging expression may help the transition to the point where pupils take the initiative.

But for the moment our pupils do not really trust us, and are not taking the bait. 'Alors, qu'est-ce qu'elle aime faire, croyez-vous?' Still no answer. Much scanning of the text reveals that 'Elle aime faire' plus noun or noun phrase does not appear.

The possibilities are still too open for our pupils to be confident of what is required. We must therefore narrow the range of choices progressively until we obtain a response.

– Elle aime jouer . . .?

We need to go further.

– Elle aime jouer au . . . au t . . .?

Let us not go the whole way, for this road leads to disappointment. Let us try shock tactics instead.

– Elle aime jouer au Rugby n'est-ce pas!

This may break the ice. Someone may be sufficiently indignant to protest, 'Non, elle aime jouer au tennis.'

But there are also other ways forward. We may use a double question.

– Elle aime jouer aux cartes, ou elle aime jouer au tennis?
– Qu'est-ce que vous croyez?

We still have the recourse of yes/no questions if this fails.

– Elle aime jouer au tennis, peut-être? Oui ou non?

Or we may try a quite different tack.

– Alors, regardez Pauline. (Holding up the book and pointing this time.)

– Qu'est-ce qu'elle tient à la main?
– Qu'est-ce que c'est alors?

We may use a combination of double questions and yes/no questions to establish that it is 'une raquette de tennis'.

– Donc, elle va jouer au . . .?

Once we are in business on this point it is then necessary to backtrack, asking different pupils, along the line of increasing generality.

– Elle aime jouer . . .?
– Qu'est-ce qu'elle aime *faire* Susan?
– Alors, dites-moi quelque chose sur Pauline, John.

In the end we are trying to train our class to respond to this kind of very open stimulus, and eventually to no stimulus at all. It may take some time, but it is worth waiting for the satisfaction of presenting a text or recording and just having one's class take off with only occasional prodding and structuring from oneself. 'Alors, qui va me dire quelque chose?' The closely structured line of questioning, however, remains necessary for bad days or for use with parts of the text which present particular difficulties of comprehension.

Each text or recording presents its own difficulties, and skilful language teachers, like the language-conscious mothers of young children, have many devices for finding out whether a particular word or expression is understood:

– Quel est le contraire de . . .?
– Donnez-moi une autre expression pour . . .?
– Qu'est-ce qu'on fait avec . . .?
– Quand est-ce qu'on porte . . . cherche . . . voit . . .?
– Comment s'appelle un homme qui . . .?

A correct answer will normally indicate that the expression is understood, as well as providing some practice in meaningful if not actually communicative speech. Confirmation by the teacher will reassure the pupil that his tentative hypothesis as to meaning was correct. If Pauline is said to be walking 'lentement' towards the bus-stop the reply that the opposite of 'lentement' is 'vite' will normally reassure the teacher that 'lentement' is understood and the teacher's confirmation will reassure the pupil that his intelligent guess or dim recollection was correct. Were Pauline carrying 'sa crosse' on the way to a hockey match, the reply that you play with it, or hit the ball with it (and confirmation by the teacher) would serve a similar function. The class would know that the object in question was the hockey stick and not something to be worn, or eaten at half-time. If she were said to be carrying 'un pamplemousse' or 'une trousse de maquillage' the replies would serve to disconfirm the hypothesis that these terms were the French for a hockey stick and might require further structured questioning to arrive at their actual meaning. Pupils' failure to provide the correct reply, or volunteer any reply at all naturally directs us towards more supportive questions which make the pupils' task easier.

As we saw, these include questions which are more specific or provide part of the answer, alternative questions and ultimately yes/no questions, if necessary with a non-verbal indication of which of the two possibilities is the right one. As will readily be seen, questions of these last two kinds have the advantage that even wrong answers by the class, when rejected by the teacher, provided pupils with the information they need to comprehend the text.

It will be unnecessary to develop the presentation of the remainder of this passage in great detail. Readers will easily envisage the possible ramifications of lines of questioning which begin by asking what one needs to play tennis, how one might carry one's kit to the venue, when and where Pauline plays, how she gets there and so on.

Needless to say, this banal little text has not been studied for the sake of its own linguistic content alone but so that we can ask our pupils parallel questions about their own weekend activities. For many teachers it will be of genuine interest – and it is important that they convey this interest – to know which pupils play for school or local sides, which go dancing or belong to various clubs, which share their parents' interest in racing pigeons, steam-engines, rabbit-breeding or whatever.

Since the vocabulary for the pupils' activities, unlike that for Pauline's is not provided by the text, double questions and other devices which feed in the information in a fairly professional and unobtrusive manner without recourse to the mother tongue will be much in demand. It will also be unnecessary to stress the importance of writing new material on the blackboard, or whatever is used in its stead, as an aid to recognition and memory and as a way of reassuring the class that they will, if they wish, have the opportunity of noting down words and phrases related to their own communicative needs at the end of this part of the lesson.

This rather teacher-centred style of work should not be continued for too long as it may easily become stressful and tedious. Questions need to be fluently produced and of an appropriate level of difficulty. A balance needs to be struck between stretching the class intellectually and keeping the lesson flowing smoothly. One must be patient and persistent while progress continues to be made, but it is often better to abandon a line of questioning than to allow it to become tortuous or agonising.

Such work is no more than preparation for the more obviously and genuinely communicative activity such as group work or pair work in which pupils ask and tell each other what they do at weekends, or commit this information to paper in a variety of letters, surveys or other writing tasks.

THE DISTRIBUTION OF QUESTIONS

Some comments should perhaps be made about the distribution of questions, which is not always as effective as it might be. There are certainly teachers who, having asked a question in the language, become so anxious at the ensuing silence that they gratefully accept the very first offer of a reply, or feel obliged to reward the first hand up by allowing its owner to answer. It is sometimes desirable to show appreciation of enthusiasm. Sometimes, too, where the answer is low-level information or is known only to one or two individuals, it may be appropriate to accept the first offer of a reply without more ado. Obviously, one wishes pupils to give some indication of their readiness to reply for this is valuable, if not entirely reliable, information about what our pupils know and understand, or think they know and understand.

In principle, however, providing the teacher with information should be regarded as the *only* purpose for which pupils raise their hands.

The policy of offering one's questions only to those who volunteer a reply, and particularly to those who regularly do so first, is disastrous for it rapidly opens up a gap between the keen and able, whose correct replies are rewarded and whose misconceptions are promptly corrected, and those who sit sullenly at the back and are soon left behind.

To accept replies only from those who offer also deprives one of a great deal of valuable information. John Bright puts up his hand and his reply shows that he has fully grasped the point. But whoever doubted that he would? What we want to know is how much the rest of the class have understood.

If the grading of our work is right we shall constantly be in doubt as to just how much is understood. Our aim is not continually to practise what is clearly within everyone's range, but constantly to raise our pupils to new levels of achievement. We therefore constantly need to ascertain that they are still with us, whether they have grasped the present point or whether there are misunderstandings to be resolved before we can proceed.

In respect of any question framed in a class-teaching situation we may hypothetically divide our class into three categories:

(A) Those who, if given the chance, would respond correctly and with ease.

(B) Those who may respond correctly, but for whom this would represent a definite achievement or reinforce something that the pupil was not previously too sure of.

(C) Those who will almost certainly be defeated by the question.

Which pupils fall into which category is, of course, entirely a matter of hypothesis, and there is an obvious danger that one will underestimate the capacities of some pupils. One therefore needs to be prepared to revise one's estimate of a pupil's capacity upwards at the slightest indication that this is appropriate. Our pupils are learning and growing all the time, and this process does not proceed at an even rate.

The proportion of pupils falling into categories A, B and C are not constant, but will clearly vary widely depending on the question. At certain points, such as when introducing new material or a new structure, we may be in some doubt as to whether anyone at all will be able to answer our first probing or open-ended questions. At this stage our class consists of a few Bs and the remainder are Cs. At other times we may ask simple focusing or refocusing questions which make few linguistic demands; or having taught a particular point we may ask a question which everyone must be able to answer if we are to be satisfied that our current objective has been achieved. We hope we have a class of As at this point.

To whom does one address one's question? Where will it be most effective? In principle, surely, though this may be subject to variation in special circumstances, one asks the pupil who just *may* give a more or less satisfactory response (a 'B'). This is for three reasons:

1. A response by this pupil will tell us more than if we had addressed the question to a pupil whom we confidently and correctly regarded as falling into category A or C (though we might, of course, have received a surprise in either case).
2. Little is achieved, except the embarrassment of the pupil concerned, by asking someone who patently cannot reply (a 'C')
3. The easy and confident reply of an 'A' on the other hand, leaves us nothing to add or develop.

Repetition by other pupils is then the only possibility remaining open before moving on to the next point. But a 'B' who is on the point of replying or has half the answer may be nudged, cajoled, encouraged, corrected. The question may be offered to someone else to complete, clues given and so on. An element of interest, suspense and cooperation is created and the class remains with the point for long enough for more and more to become interested and to understand.

Our strategy may, of course, not be entirely successful. The selected pupil may reply adequately right away, so that from his point of view nothing remains to be said. The temptation is to assume all is well, and pass on to the next point. Those who did not know the answer will have heard it and now be in the picture, we suppose.

This is, to say the least, somewhat optimistic. One right answer proves nothing and we should be well advised to offer the same question to one of the weaker members of the form either now or in a few minutes' time. The last thing we want to encourage is the belief that a question that is being answered by someone else may safely be ignored because, like yesterday's date, it will never return.

But suppose we receive no reply from our chosen pupil? Though it is often appropriate, indeed important, to allow a certain thinking time as well as offer support and encouragement, it is important not to agonise or leave the pupil in a state of tortured captivity for what to him may seem an eternity. It is also rarely profitable simply to repeat the question, especially if one does so in a louder, threatening or exasperated tone of voice. There is no quicker way to reduce a class to stammering inarticulacy. One needs to switch the question quickly to another pupil, also in the 'B' category for this question. If a satisfactory answer is obtained, it is essential to return briefly to the one who originally failed, to allow him to show that he too now understands the point. If our second pupil also fails to respond satisfactorily we may well wish to turn to someone who we think probably will respond satisfactorily before, of course, briefly allowing those who failed to do so to rehabilitate themselves.

As mentioned, there may be occasions when we do not direct our questions to those whom we regard as lying in the B category with regard to the question concerned. In introducing new material or aiming to encourage use of a particular structure we may prefer to make use of a pupil who we think will get us off to a good start or provide a good model for others to follow. On the other hand, especially with a temporarily cocky or inattentive class,we may wish to pull them up short by asking a question that we expect most people to be unable to answer. In this case, of course, we must rehabilitate and reassure our 'victim' as soon as possible.

Some questions will be intended to stretch our ablest pupils and may not be addressed to the remainder of the class at all. Others will concern more fundamental points which cannot be left until all members of the class are in a position to respond to them satisfactorily. The overriding and most general principle in teaching, as in other practical activities, is to be efficient and economical. In the present context this means not wasting questions on those who will not profit from attempting to answer them. This is particularly important in the case of certain simple questions which the flow and structure of our lesson may make necessary. These are a precious resource to be reserved for those of our pupils who are capable of responding satisfactorily to these questions only. Needless to say the relatively limited number of satisfactory responses these pupils are able to make are also precious, and are to be received with due and in no way insincere signs of appreciation.

REVIEW AND ENHANCEMENT

1. Consider a unit which it is proposed to study in the near future.
   (a) Identify or produce a text or recording containing new language essential to the unit.
   (b) Identify the cultural and linguistic objectives you would hope to achieve by use of the material.
   (c) Identify any likely difficulties of comprehension and prepare general lines of questioning.
   (d) Mentally revise the functions of: focusing questions or instructions, double questions, yes/no questions, open-ended and more specific questions, testing questions. Mentally revise correction techniques and procedures for dealing with failure to respond.
   (e) Decide upon an appropriate amount of time for presenting the material to the class. Make a recording of your presentation.
2. Study your recording of the previous activity.
   (a) Evaluate the quality of the class's response over the period of the activity as a whole. If this was less than entirely satisfactory try to say whether this was because: (i) questions were too easy to stimulate pupils to reply: (ii) questions were too hard so that they were not understood, or required answers pupils were unable to produce; (iii) your own questioning technique lacked ease and fluency and failed to inspire confidence; (iv) pupils were unused to this way of working. Formulate any relevant amendments to your techique for further use.
   (b) Consider whether you adequately capitalised on what pupils already knew or understood. Were your questions distributed in the most profitable and economical way?
   (c) Identify any awkward silences or points at which you were obliged to revert to English or engage in explanation instead of questioning. Assess whether these could have been avoided by use of any of the questioning techniques described in the chapter.
   (d) Attempt to assess whether the cultural or linguistic objectives were achieved. Identify pupil responses on the tape which justify this belief.
3. Attempt to categorise your questions (e.g. focusing questions, open-ended questions, double questions, yes/no questions, rephrasing questions (more specific/less specific than the previous one) repeated questions, testing questions.
   (a) Log your question types during short sections of the activity. Note how different types of questions are distributed over the period of the activity as a whole, and also

any recurring sequences of question types. Assess the desirability or usefulness of these with a view to enhancing future practice.

(b) Repeat the above review processes periodically. Retain earlier recordings for comparison. Note any developments and improvements over time.

FURTHER READING

McNair J (1973) 'Putting the question', *Modern Languages*, **54** (1), 27–31

Perrott E 1982 *Effective Teaching*. Longman, London, pp 41–54

Wringe C A 1976 *Developments in Modern Language Teaching*. Open Books, London, pp 25–35

Wringe C A 1977 'The use of interaction analysis and micro-teaching in the training of modern language teachers', *NALA Journal*, **8** 40–44

CHAPTER 7

Differentiation in years 1–5

One of the commonest causes of unsatisfactory classroom relationships, and consequently of ineffective teaching, is failure to take due account of the group or individual one is dealing with. The imaginative role-play that went so well with one's chirpy new first-formers may completely fail with a sullen group in the fourth, especially if they think that by asking them to engage in some form of make-believe one is showing insufficient regard for their dignity. Not only do groups differ according to age but also according to ability and motivation. Mixed-ability groups will need to be treated differently from relatively homogeneous sets from whatever part of the ability range. Though classes may often have their own distinctive group personality, individuals within them will also vary widely in their capacity and response. The generalisations I am bound to make in what follows must therefore necessarily be treated with caution.

STARTING THEM OFF

The peculiar characteristics of first-formers or indeed beginners of any age are frequently overlooked. There is a great temptation to skim rapidly over the opening stages of the course, either on the grounds that this is all terribly simple or that there will be plenty of time to revise whatever is not fully grasped later on, on the apparent assumption that learning is learning is learning, no matter when or by whom it is done. One German course which was very widely used until quite recently offered 30 new words to be learned in the first unit, exactly as in every other unit, right the way through to the end of the fifth form.

In some situations, no doubt, there is wisdom in the adage that one should begin as one means to go on. In an educational context, however, it is difficult to think of anything more crass. What may seem obvious or even tedious to old hands in the second year will be shatteringly new to first-time second-language learners, especially during their first few weeks. What is important is not to 'get away to a flying start' for there is plenty of time ahead of us. In any case, a sound beginning will pay dividends by enabling more rapid and trouble-free progress to be made later on. Subsequent confusion and disheartenment may well have its source in a lack of sensitivity during this early period when everything is new and potentially overwhelming.

The priority in this early stage is to gain the confidence of the class and to familiarise them with one's way of working. A first lesson or so in which not a great deal of language is introduced but in which pupils are invited to discuss anything they know about the country whose language they are to learn (either from holiday visits or at second hand) is invaluable for this purpose. It also provides an opportunity for the teacher to get to know pupils individually before more intensive work gets under way.

It is also important that one should not introduce too much content at this early stage. For a time, beginners (even those who have learned other foreign languages) are extremely tolerant of repetition and a return to what was done, however intensively, yesterday or the day before is welcomed as an opportunity to show that one really has mastered it, and will certainly not be rejected as boring. Mastery is always a pleasing experience and nothing is so boring as skimming from point to point without having the time to possess any of them fully.

Despite newer communicative aims which stress that perfect imitation of the native speaker is not required and places value on gist comprehension even though some parts of a text or recording may not be followed at all, it is not clear that beginners and near-beginners ought to be given material which they do not fully understand or master (but see Page 1986). With the most careful presentation in the world, misunderstandings and confusions both about the meaning of individual words and about how the language functions are bound to arise and it is perverse to add to the problems and anxieties of this initial phase unnecessarily. In particular, it is important to anticipate and control the transition from repetition to independent use, from speech to writing and from copy-writing to recall and, eventually, independent production.

If these very important stages are handled sensitively a bond of confidence is built up between teacher and pupils. Pupils come to know that even if there are temporary uncertainties they and the teacher between them have the situation under control and they will not be left floundering in the long run. On this basis it becomes possible to move ahead more rapidly and confidently once the initial phase is complete. This 'opening up' as pupils become confident in handling more and more unfamiliar material, or able to use new words and phrases with progressively less rehearsal proceeds steadily through the later part of the first year and during the second.

THE MIDDLE YEARS

In contrast to the first year, many new teachers typically find their second- and third-year groups the most difficult to deal with. No doubt puberty and other more general problems of adolescence have much to do with this. Factors connected with the way the language course naturally develops at this stage, however, may make the teacher's task more difficult and bestow even greater importance on the development of satisfactory personal and classroom relationships with pupils in the middle years. Even in supposedly streamed or setted groups there may, at this stage, be wide differences not only of attainment but, more importantly, of maturity and motivation. Pupils' interests and aspirations may fluctuate back and forth. One day a pupil may still be the 'good child' like a first-former keen to have the teacher's approval. The next he, or she, may be more interested in peer-group approval for a show of defiance and then, maddeningly, resentful at the 'unfairness' of the teacher who speaks harshly or shows impatience.

The task of growing up is necessarily a perplexing one. It is, for example, not always clear how much responsibility one is expected to take upon oneself for one's work or behaviour. If one behaves badly, is one being childish? If one does not, is one being a wimp? How much can one get away with? How far dare one push one's luck? Maybe one may sometimes protest at unreasonable amounts of homework, or at being moved around too much or asked to do silly things. But when, exactly, is this permissible? Adolescents can only learn the answers to these questions by trial, error and experiment in a confusing social world in which adult responses may be far from consistent.

For this reason it is customary in some schools to ensure that wherever possible the middle forms are taught by experienced members of staff who are not in any way in doubt about their own identity. What is required at this stage more than any other is firmness, consistency and sometimes even a degree of formality. One needs to move easily between a relaxed, informal working activity and a brisker, more formal manner when it is necessary to bring enthusiasm back under control or move on to something new without loss of time. Above all, one needs to signal the required change unambiguously to the class.

At this stage more than any other, careful preparation is required, for unlike both older and younger groups second- and third-formers make few allowances for activities that go wrong, and are quick to ridicule any form of ineptness. The use of straightforward, predictable routines whose purpose is self-evident and which do not need too much discussion will generally be welcomed by pupils. So too will be the insistence on good order, acceptable behaviour, adequate standards of effort and homework properly done on time. A good clear indication of what is and what is not on avoids a great deal of uncertainty and anxiety. For if it is known that a teacher simply will not tolerate certain shortcomings one may conform without loss of face, in the knowledge that only the foolish would do otherwise.

This is in no way intended as a defence of any repressive or authoritarian regime. The task is not to prolong the relationship of dependency in which younger pupils may stand to their teachers but, on the contrary, progressively to liberate them from childhood.

While indicating clearly what is acceptable it is equally important to support and show appreciation for initiative, imagination and genuine efforts to do the right thing responsibly and independently. Failure to do this may leave pupils downcast and alienated, and if one too often comes across rather sullen, disaffected fourth-year groups it may well be that the policy of 'taking a firm line' has been applied without judgement or discrimination.

In this section, we have devoted some attention to the general development of 13–14-year-olds because of the great importance of understanding the outlook of one's pupils and getting one's classroom relationships right at this stage. This is not only for wider educational reasons but because of the particular demands of language teaching in the central years of the five-year course.

Despite the relatively wide differences of attainment that will have opened up in all groups by this stage, even relatively ungifted pupils will by now have gained a good stock of language experience, as well as strategies for coping with gaps in that experience. To take advantage of this, and maintain a sense of gradation and growing mastery, pupils need a regime of varied, flexible and increasingly independent work. Clearly this need cannot be met unless one has the cooperation and goodwill of all individuals in the class.

This age-group is not without its special compensations. Despite its patchy appearance, some pupils at this stage will have begun to show the beginnings of maturity and a readiness to take responsibility for their own progress. The ablest and most enthusiastic will work through an enormous amount of material. For these pupils the greater the challenge, the more positive the response. This potential needs to be recognised and responded to, for if it is not, much energy and enthusiasm is likely to be channelled into other directions, not all of them educationally beneficial.

The third year also sees the beginnings of adult interests and an adult perspective. It is now seriously possible for pupils to envisage ordering a meal or driving a car in the foreign country as a reality and no longer as a kind of fairy-tale make-believe game for the teacher's benefit. This sense of the reality of the foreign country and its language will be aided by the fact that some pupils will have experienced life in the country through the school's exchange scheme.

For many pupils the growing psychological orientation towards adulthood will bring the foreseeable prospect of leaving school and entering the world, if not of work, then at least of semi-adult responsibilities and preoccupations. This has important implications for the materials we use. If our pupils are not to see what we do in the classroom as something of little interest, since it is soon to be left behind, the content of our materials and lessons must reflect those preoccupations. Access to a good supply of authentic and appropriate printed and recorded materials reflecting the interests of young people like themselves in the foreign country is therefore essential.

There is a need for a sense of gradation, not only in the growing maturity of the materials we place before our pupils but also in the tasks they are required to tackle. It is important, especially with pupils whose progress seems slow by traditional standards, that progress from term to term and year to year should not simply be a matter of passing from one topic to the next – quite apart from the fact that, by the third year, entirely new topics may be in rather short supply. Having listened to recordings in the first form to find out whether customers want to buy apples or pears it is not necessarily any form of progression to listen to similar recordings in the fourth to find out whether motorists wish to buy *ordinaire* or *super* or change their money for traveller's cheques or cash. The material in which the required information is embedded needs to be of greater length and complexity, and comprehension needs to depend on more previously acquired knowledge of the language. This is the only way in which such previously acquired knowledge can be kept alive. If each new topic represents a new beginning, there is little motivation to hang on to what is learned, since it is unlikely that it will be required again. As well as having greater linguistic experience and more coping skills, pupils will also have more experience of customs and practices in the adult world and more can be taken for granted regarding what will or will not be implicitly understood. Where there is doubt as to what is or is not understood, it is highly desirable to refrain from straightforward explanations 'to be on the safe side'. A judicious question whose purpose is not obvious will indicate the extent of the class's knowledge, and the reply may serve to inform the less sophisticated.

It is during the middle years that the so-called 'four skills' begin to develop independently, and at different rates. During the early stages one may hesitate to introduce too much material which is not fully understood and mastered, but even as the first year gets under way, what can be read and understood aurally begins conspicuously to outstrip what can be said, written or even accurately copied.

This process continues through the second year and into the third, so that it becomes increasingly important to ensure that all of the skills are being developed to the fullest possible extent. This is partly a question of the even allocation of time. Many authentic activities are, of course, of a multi-skill variety and a formal division between listening, reading, speaking and writing may be neither possible nor desirable. Nevertheless, a degree of informal self-monitoring may make one aware that one or other of the skills is receiving less than its fair share of attention. This is particularly important where there are factors tending to distort the pattern of one's teaching activity. With a particularly difficult or lively class one may instinctively avoid speaking activities. On the other hand, shortage of suitable materials or unfavourable conditions may cause one to neglect one or other of the receptive skills.

Allocation of time is only part of the story, however. Even if time is being allocated more or less equally to the four skills, it may still be the case that while progress is being made in one or two, the class is coasting in others. Longer and more complex reading passages may be rapidly extending the range of what pupils can comprehend, while speaking activities remain at the level of predictable and stereotyped transactions. What is even more likely is that whereas pupils are being pushed to improve their performance in productive skills of speaking and writing where progress or shortcomings are highly visible, their potential for progress in the receptive skills is being under-utilised.

In the area of speaking it obviously becomes important that the tasks pupils have to carry out should show an increase in complexity and require more extended speech. Efforts need to be made to ensure that required responses should be increasingly unpredictable, so that some approach is made to real-life situations.

Not only may hotel owners offer an alternative if the required room with bath and balcony overlooking the sea is not available, but bakers may pass comment on the weather or admire the customer's new hat instead of asking how many rolls are required. In both speaking and writing the principle of progression requires that pupils should be steadily weaned off teacher's guidance in the selection of what is to be said. Though much material may be presented and practised in preparation for writing an enquiry about holiday facilities, it is important that progressively at this stage, responsibility for deciding how much to say or how detailed enquiries may reasonably be made should fall to the pupils. It is therefore important that current concern with specific objectives and the establishment of detailed assessment criteria should not inhibit progress towards the pupils' exercise of independent judgement and the development of social as well as linguistic skills.

It is sometimes suggested that when pupils are self-conscious, unsure of themselves and frightened of losing face, this is the time to concentrate on the receptive skills in which one's performance is less public. Rapid and exciting progress in the receptive skills is often possible both because of pupils' increasing stock of linguistic knowledge and rapidly growing interest in the outside world. Accessible materials may be of genuine interest to the teacher as well as to pupils. The switch to work on the receptive skills – especially work on individual reading comprehension assignments may also reduce class-control problems.

Clearly there is sense in the suggestion that the moment of readiness should be exploited to the full and that if this is the point at which pupils become capable of coping with a wider range of reading and listening materials, and are enthusiastic to do so, the opportunity should not be missed. Nevertheless, it is an essential educative task to help pupils pass through the stage of adolescent self-consciousness into one of adult poise and self-confidence, rather than encourage the lapse into mutism to which many are prone. Rather than avoid productive, especially speaking, tasks it is therefore suggested that we should continue to work on these in due proportion as before, firmly but supportively, with due regard for the sensitivities of individuals.

THE EXAMINATION YEAR

Under the traditional regime the fifth year was often unsatisfactory from a teaching point of view. Even where progressive methods were used in earlier years, it was often felt necessary, by both teachers and pupils, to abandon these in favour of examination practice in formal translation, essays of strictly determined length, picture compositions, aural comprehension tests, rehearsing the all-important 'hundred questions' and so on.

To some extent the problem is alleviated under the new GSCE arrangements in so far as the objectives which the examination purports to test are those of the course as a whole. Nevertheless, some fairly specific examination preparation, different in kind from the best teaching practice earlier in the course, may still be appropriate if pupils are to do justice to themselves in the examination. Tasks set for the purposes of assessment cannot be too open-ended or rely too heavily on individual interpretation or initiative. They must be capable of accomplishment within a fairly predictable and limited time-span. The intelligent use of reference books and other sources of material is not allowed in examinations, nor is mature and sensible cooperation or consultation with others.

As things stand, examination tasks must be designed to test individual language skills, for which purpose multi-skill activities are ruled out as, by definition, unsuitable. It nevertheless remains important, especially during the first term of the examination year, to avoid 'staleness' and a feeling of unbroken examination grind by continuing to introduce new, stimulating and varied work for as long as possible.

As the examination approaches, and certainly after any 'mock' examinations have taken place, pupils will be relatively resistant to new material or activities which they feel to be substantially different from those likely to be encountered in the examination. The primary interest will be in ensuring that they can cope with the anticipated tasks in the examination. This can be put to obvious pedagogic use, for at this point pupils are fairly happy to repeat certain key tasks over and over again in various guises. Familiarity which earlier gave rise to boredom and rejection is now welcome and reassuring. Pupils may also be more disposed than previously to pay attention to matters of detail. This need not signal a reversion to the traditional preoccupation with minor points of verbal or adjectival agreement and so on. We may, however, now be in a position to tighten up on a number of points that have gone unheeded for too long. We may now more effectively insist that pupils express themselves clearly and articulately with the language at their disposal. Ambiguities of pronunciation which might plausibly impede communication may be put right if this has not already been done, and efforts can be made to end undue reliance on the sympathies (and telepathic skills) of the native speaker. In the area of receptive skills, pupils who have tended to adopt a somewhat approximate approach to what they heard and saw, may now be encouraged to read and listen more carefully and pay more precise attention to the information they are required to extract.

If there is one particular requirement of effective teaching in this final year, however, it is at all costs to avoid playing on pupils' examination fears as a means of motivation. Frequently this is not done with any rational aim of increasing pupils' effort and attention but simply results from the teacher allowing his or her own anxiety to communicate itself to the pupils. On the whole, those pupils who are likely to be motivated by the examination are already perfectly well aware of its approach and its importance for them. To increase the level of anxiety is not only inhumane, but may also undermine whatever spontaneous and non-instrumental interest the pupil may take in the subject.

DIFFERENTIATION BY ABILITY

One of the great advantages of GCSE-style language examinations is that it is now possible to set and reward tasks valid for
pupils over the full range of ability from the earliest weeks of the
course. Under the traditional regime, even the achievements of
relatively able fifth-formers were of little practical, intellectual or
aesthetic value, since all but a few of the relatively small segment
of the ability range who studied foreign languages found the task
of producing grammatical or even coherent work in the language
beyond them.

The remainder were defined as 'non-linguistic' not because
they were incapable of acquiring language but because the ways
in which language was taught and tested defeated them. It may
be added that the achievements of even the ablest were relatively
trivial. In so far as grammatical accuracy and the imitation of
native speech were the criteria of success, most pupils simply
learned that they were 'no good at languages'.

Happily it is now possible to find valid achievements of an
appropriate level all the way across the ability range. In contrast
to the often incoherent renderings of banal English narratives or
barbarous English versions of literary or subliterary texts in the
foreign language, understanding simple announcements, notices
and messages, making lists and even copy-writing and giving brief
oral responses are all valid and useful achievements at even the
most elementary level.

Some people may see in this change a danger that many of the
ablest linguists will be intellectually under-extended. Under the
traditional regime, pupils had to wrestle with grammatical rules
and structures of some complexity, attend to matters of detail
and perform demanding feats of memory and analysis. For some
there was also the challenge of literary or subliterary extensive
reading of works intended for adult readers of some sophisti-
cation. In a small number of pupils these tasks inspired enormous
dedication, and such pupils are unimpressed by easy options.

If language teaching is to be a valid educational experience for
all pupils it must continue to extend the ablest while at the same
time providing an appropriate degree of stimulation and challenge for others. Theoretically, this should not be a problem. If
there are notices, messages and other things to read that are very
simple (*Danger*!, *Silence*!) there are certainly texts that are
complex and difficult – technical, literary and academic texts are
obvious examples. While some situations demand simple stereotyped responses, others may require carefully composed
speech or flexible reactions to the responses of others. The range
of possible writing tasks and the variation in the amount of
support and guidance given, are limitless.

Appropriate tasks must be devised for pupils of different abilities and, if other educational aspirations are not to go by the board, this may need to be done in classes containing pupils of a wide range of ability. It is no longer possible or thought educationally desirable to select out able pupils at an early stage and give them a special academic course with little chance of later transfer in to or out of the main stream (cf. HMI 1977: 49). Even if this were possible, furthermore, it would not solve the problem for even supposedly homogeneous groups may contain pupils of a considerable range or ability, so that need for differentiation within the group remains.

Besides providing valid objectives for the main part of the ability range, new syllabuses also make it easier to deal with a wider range of ability in a number of ways.

Although different levels of examination are offered in the four skills, there is no obvious discontinuity in the demands made on those who are to take basic and those who are to take higher level tests. Those taking the higher level have to do essentially the same sort of thing as those taking basic only, but over a rather wider range of language and contexts, as well, of course, as also completing the 'basic' tests themselves. There should, therefore, be no need to rigidly select into 'basic' and 'higher' streams, as was the case when separate General Certificate of Education (GCE) and Certificate of Secondary Education (CSE) examinations were taken. Having pupils taking higher and those taking basic level only in a particular skill should not, therefore, prove disastrous and is in fact likely to be the case in most classes.

It is also of advantage that courses are no longer based on grammatical progression as was the case even with enlightened direct or oral method approaches and most audio-visual courses. In such courses it was necessary for the whole class to master a particular structure before the next step was undertaken. Failure to do this would lead to confusion and constant frustration later on, especially as it was felt that grammatical errors *always* had to be corrected. An all but universal axiom of good teaching was to work hard to keep one's bottom end up, to keep one's group together and as far as possible to avoid allowing anyone to get left behind.

The teacher is now freed from such lock-step requirements and may exercise his professional judgement as to what it is or is not appropriate to insist upon in the case of individual pupils.

At a particular point he may, for example, be faced with the decision as to what to do about the distinction between *au* and *à la*, where pupils are producing for example *il va au* boulangerie, il va à la* cinéma* fairly indiscriminately. Under the old regime everything had to stop at once. The error could not be allowed to pass and if it was thought that there was any doubt as to the principle involved, the whole thing had to be explained again, with paradigmatic examples of the various forms being written on the blackboard and possibly copied down into everyone's exercise books – even by those who were already thoroughly competent in their use. This was often excruciatingly time-wasting for the ablest who often grasped the principle as soon as it was stated, and unhelpful to others who really needed the explanation but were thrown by the terms (singular, feminine, vowel, etc.) in which it was couched.

In the new situation there will certainly be individuals and groups of pupils for whom such explanations, whether given in formal terms or built up inductively, are perfectly valid. Explanation may be a quick and efficient way of improving the quality of oral communication, and should not be withheld. For others, use of what is recognisably part of the verb 'to go' in connection with various buildings and other destinations may already be an achievement, and recognition of this may be more important than gilding the lily by insisting on the distinction between *au* and *à la*, failure to observe which only marginally detracts from smooth communication.

The principle of differentiation also demands that we set different pupils different tasks. Previously, though it was often prudent to offer more difficult questions to pupils of known ability in the first instance, they would soon be repeated for the benefit of others. What was expected of one was expected of all. This was always unkind and unreasonable, necessarily defining all but the ablest as being in deficit. In mixed-ability or even broadly banded classes it becomes obviously inappropriate.

There is, of course, an important caveat. Where the same is not demanded of all pupils present in a particular classroom, the teacher's individual judgement and expectations will determine what is demanded of any individual pupil and this, in turn, may influence that pupil's rate of progress. It is therefore necessary to guard against unduly low expectations of certain categories of pupils, especially when these are relatively taciturn and disinclined to trouble those who do not trouble them.

The setting of different tasks to different pupils does not have to take place all the time. When a new topic or even a new function is first introduced, a great deal of what is presented may be new to all pupils and the presentation may be in relatively simple terms without boring the most competent. In certain kinds of group work such as the composing of dialogues or cooperative work on reading comprehension tasks, the more able will naturally tend to do the lion's share of the work. This does not mean that others will swing the lead or fail to extend themselves.

On the contrary, they are likely to compete to put their two-penn'orth in, for pupils who accept their teacher's definition of them as 'dim' and sit passively in class are by no means as ready to do so when working with their peers. Nor is there a great deal of truth in the gibe that such activity holds back the able who are obliged to help their slower classmates along. In the cooperative activity all contribute what they can and learn accordingly. The only requirement is that the activity should at least contain something that is sufficiently demanding for the ablest in the groups to be fully stretched in the joint performance.

The setting of differentiated assignments is not as difficult or time-consuming as many traditional teachers have assumed, though it does have important resourcing and timetabling implications. When it was thought that effective learning could only be achieved as a result of constant correction by the teacher, all activity had to be teacher-centred and class teaching was probably the most efficient arrangement – hence the long-standing resistance of many modern linguists to mixed-ability teaching and the clear suggestion by some that in modern languages, mixed-ability teaching was a less than ideal arrangement (Walmsey 1975: 190–201). To provide for even three different levels meant teaching one-third of the pupils at a time, while giving the rest something to get on with. Precious contact time was divided by three as far as the pupil was concerned, so one felt obliged to get as much into 10 minutes as one had previously covered in 30. One had to prepare three lessons instead of one and teaching was stressful as one constantly had to break off to discipline those told to get on under their own steam. There was also bound to be a great deal of extra marking since what was written without proper supervision and preparation was inevitably full of mistakes.

From the point of view of differentiation the move to communicative objectives has the great advantage of releasing both teachers and pupils from a regime in which everything written or said by any pupil had to be controlled and checked by the teacher. Much class teaching remains, of course. In addition to the presentation and discussion of new topics, the giving of models and listening to and discussing pupils' efforts may be helpful to all members of the class. But there are many communicative activities which, provided they are sensibly set up in the first place, do not need continual and detailed monitoring. A piece of reading or listening comprehension in the language laboratory may properly occupy a class for, say 15–20 minutes and success may be monitored by a few short questions to which the answers are given by one or two judiciously selected individuals. Even speaking activities in groups or pairs need only be

fairly loosely monitored to deal with such problems as misunderstanding or undue excitability which may arise from time to
time.

The use of communicative methods in class, plus the fact that
pupils of a wide range of ability produce considerably less written
work than their predecessors in homogeneous and relatively able
sets, means that the weekly chore of marking is nowadays much
reduced. The teacher is consequently much freer, both in the
classroom and in whatever time he devotes to school work after
hours, to devise a variety of activities and vary them as becomes
necessary in the course of the lesson.

Once it is realized that this extra breathing-space is available,
parts of the language teacher's day become rather like that of the
teacher of other practical subjects. He is no longer perpetually
'giving out', gripping and dominating the class by the sheer force
of his personality, but is able to think in terms of 'managing' the
work of his pupils, choosing tasks for individuals, ensuring that
those who finish quickly have extra work to do, exempting some
from elementary tasks and setting more demanding ones for
others, resolving individual problems and so on. Extra tasks for
the ablest may include extensive reading for interest, longer or
more advanced reading comprehension pieces in which a relatively small amount of information has to be extracted from a
good deal of other interesting material, more complex speaking
tasks to be performed by some groups, writing tasks additional
to the speaking tasks performed by other pupils and so on.
Equally, of course, it may be necessary to find simpler tasks for
the less able. Listing and labelling may take the place of more
extended writing. If providing separate comprehension materials
is sometimes too time-consuming, less able pupils can be given
a bit more guidance as to what to look or listen for before they
begin, presented with an abbreviated text and list of questions
or simply set easier questions on the same text.

Pupils in mixed-ability classes do not find it at all invidious that
some are given harder or easier tasks than others and are accustomed to this practice from other subjects, and from the primary
school. Those who are just coping are glad not to be given more
to do, and the ablest enjoy the challenge of more demanding
work.

The provision of tests of different levels in the examination is
thought to be necessary in order to be able to set appropriate
tasks to pupils over the full range of ability. It is not yet clear
how this provision will affect the timetabling and grouping of
pupils in the long run. Hopefully, it will not lead to pupils being
rigidly divided into higher and basic sets and certainly not into
higher and basic *streams* across the whole curriculum at an early
stage. There is little justification for this in languages. Not only

are the skills required for higher tests continuous with those needed at basic level but there also exists the possibility of taking the higher tests in some of the four skills and the basic only in others. Hopefully the principle of mixed-ability teaching with increasingly diversified individual assignments will be preserved throughout most if not all of the five-year course. It is equally desirable that choices between higher and basic tests should be regarded as last-minute decisions of examination strategy rather than as choices about what course a pupil is to follow. Ideally, the question of what tasks a particular pupil is to be set tomorrow should be determined in the light of his ability and readiness, not by detailed study of the examination requirements for this level or that. Language teachers should, indeed, guard against acquiring too close and detailed a knowledge of their examination syllabus, or they may find themselves operating according to such maxims as: 'This group are taking higher level, so I'd better cover this' (whether or not they are yet ready for it). Or even worse, 'They don't have to know this word for basic level, so I'd better stop them using it.'

Such attitudes are death to enthusiasm and good motivation which are the results of giving pupils tasks which *just* exceed in difficulty those which they are comfortably able to perform. The essential question, in evaluating the content of one's lesson is, firstly, whether one's main task was of the right level for the majority of the class, and then, whether there were not some pupils who required the challenge of more difficult work and others who were struggling and would therefore have profited from something on similar lines but more manageable.

REVIEW AND ENHANCEMENT

1. For purposes of comparison, make recordings of yourself carrying out broadly similar activities (presenting new language, setting homework, organising group work) with first and third years.
   (a) Consider whether there are appropriate differences of tone, manner, tolerance of uncertainties and queries from the class, assumptions about working practices and previous knowledge, etc. Consider whether you are being sufficiently careful with first forms, or doing adequate justice to the existing knowledge and independence of third forms. Review the preparation of forthcoming lessons with these considerations in mind.
   (b) Record lessons with any second-, third- or fourth-year group you regard as difficult in any way. Analyse your recording and attempt to say whether any of the following

may be partly reponsible for the uncooperative atittude of your class! (i) Insufficiently mature or demanding material. (ii) Inadequate preparation and lack of pace or decisiveness in the lesson. (iii) Provocativeness or over-anxiety on your part to dominate and control the class. (iv) Differences in attainment necessitating individual assignments. Devise ways of implementing any changes in manner or policy that seem desirable.

(c) Consider any particularly unresponsive fourth-form group you may have. Review your projected work for the next three to four weeks. Attempt to identify some authentic stimulating and sophisticated materials from outside the course. Record the first 10 minutes of two or three consecutive lessons. Rate your opening remarks and initial activity A, B or C for impact and challenge. Give particular attention to the start of your lessons in planning your next week's work, and note any improvement in the response of the class.

2. Review work currently planned for any examination class you may have.

   (a) Consider whether this adequately balances the stimulation of new work with routine revision and examination practice.

   (b) Listen to a recording of one of your lessons. Look for clear, firm correction and brisk supportive comment. Seek to eliminate any tendency to agonise over doubtful issues or to dwell upon the importance or difficulty of the examination.

3. Plan a unit of work for a third or fourth year.

   (a) Review listening and reading comprehension material to ensure that these are sufficiently extensive and demanding. Ensure that there are adequate writing activities for those who may be taking higher level writing.

   (b) Identify extensive reading and additional listening and reading comprehension materials for quicker pupils. Devise extended versions of writing activities, or versions requiring more independent judgement.

   (c) Consider suitable alternative or amended receptive skill materials and activities for the least able and prepare extra guidance or alternative writing activities. If necessary devise simplified role-play and pair-work activi-ties or be prepared to provide extra support.

   (d) Include 'differentiated work' as a heading in your lesson planning. Provisionally identify by name the pupils who are to benefit from differentiated work.

FURTHER READING

Helpful material on differentiation by either stage of ability in language teaching is relatively sparse. The following, however, contain a number of illuminating remarks.

Lafayette R C 1980 'Differentiation of language instruction', in F M Grittner (ed.), *Learning a Second Language.* ' University of Chicago Press, Chicago, pp 67–87
SEC/Open University 1986 *French*, GCSE, *A Guide for Teachers*. Open University Press, Milton Keynes, pp. 7–10
Walmsley R. S. 1975 'French', in A. V. Kelly (ed), *Case Studies in Mixed Ability Teaching*. Harper & Row, London, pp. 190–201

The GCSE National Criteria for French (DES 1985) and the GCSE language syllabuses of the various examining groups are admirably specific in their requirements for basic and higher level tests but do not, of course, attempt to give guidance on the teaching approaches suitable for different groups of pupils.

CHAPTER 8

Language teaching 16–19

THE TARGET POPULATION

Among those continuing their language studies in the sixth form or its tertiary or further education (FE) equivalents there will be a number of students seeking to take GCSE for the first time or repeating the examination in order to improve their grades. Others will be studying a language for a number of reasons without a particular examination in mind. In FE establishments students may be pursuing various vocational language qualifications, and interesting developments are taking place with regard to the 16–19 age-group in this context (Godfrey 1987).

The examining boards are also engaged in the production of A/S-level examinations. These are intended for those who wish to continue to study a foreign language beyond the level of GCSE, without devoting as much as one-third of their time to the subject, as would be required by an A-level course. It is intended that A/S-level examinations in all subjects should be of the same intellectual rigour as A level, but that syllabuses should contain significantly less material. It is expected that the amount of contact and private study time spent on an A/S course will be approximately half of that required for an A-level course. At the time of writing the Associated Examining Board (AEB) has produced an A/S-level examination syllabus in which the skills of listening, reading and speaking only will be tested. There have for some time existed various sixth-form examinations beyond the level of those taken at 16+ but less demanding than A level. These, including AO level and the Certificate of Extended Education (CEE) have, on the whole, not been taken by large numbers of students. It remains to be seen whether A/S levels will prove more attractive. To date it is not clear what the nature and size of their public will be. It is equally unclear what form effective teaching at this level must take and how, if at all, it will differ from that appropriate to A-level pupils. It is equally unclear whether numbers will justify separate A/S-level provision or whether it will prove necessary and practical to combine classes with those of A-level students.

It seems likely that, in the foreseeable future, A levels in their revised form will be the main concern of most of those teaching languages to the 16–19 age group. This being so it is appropriate to make some remarks about both the A-level target group and the revised form of the examinations themselves.

In recent years it has become increasingly clear that sixth-form language sets are by no means entirely, or even mainly, composed of future specialist linguists going on to follow traditional modern languages honours degree courses of language and literature. On the contrary, in most language sixth forms, such students will be the minority. In 1984 only some 60 per cent of students passing French at A level went on to degree courses and of those only 40 per cent (i.e. 24 per cent of the whole group) went on to degree courses with a language component. Less than half of this group (i.e. less than 12 per cent of the successful candidates as a whole) followed courses in languages only. Honours degree courses themselves, moreover, have become more varied in recent years and no longer consist solely of the traditional studies of language and literature (JMB 1984). This being so it is clear that modern language courses at A level must cater for a wide range of candidates, for the majority of whom language is not of central concern though it may provide a useful secondary skill.

In the light of these facts, and changing views of the nature and purpose of language learning, boards have undertaken substantial revisions of their A-level language syllabuses.

LANGUAGE WORK

The stated syllabus aims of the boards examining at A level refer to the ability to understand both the spoken and written language at an appropriate level as well as the ability to communicate fact, opinion and ideas in a coherent ordered way by means of appropriate written and spoken language. Recognition is also given to the part played by sixth-form studies in students' intellectual and cultural development. One board (JMB 1984) also openly avows its aim of framing its examination tests in such a way as to influence classroom teaching in directions it considers desirable. Translation from and into the foreign language continues for the moment to figure among the tests of reading comprehension and written production set by some boards, but are given much less prominence than formerly alongside other tests of the same skills. All syllabuses require study of both language itself and a body of knowledge to which the language is a principal means of access (SCUE/CNAA 1986: 1). In some cases this body of knowledge continues to be provided by the study of literature in a form more or less identical to that of the traditional A-level literature examination. In others a wider range of reading is offered. Part or all of this section of the syllabus will, in future, be examined by means of answers or essays written in the foreign language.

In the sixth form as elsewhere, effective teaching is not a matter of coaching pupils in the performance of specific tests, but of developing the basic aptitudes and capacities, often specified as the aims of the course, which make their performance possible.

If students are to perform well in tasks that depend on a ready understanding of recorded and printed material of a certain level, they must experience a good deal of material of that kind over an extended period. Likewise, if they are to use language to communicate information, ideas or opinion they need to see and hear this being done by others. They also need plenty of opportunity to attempt this task for themselves with both the freedom to experiment and find their own way of doing things and supportive and sympathetic guidance from a teacher who is familiar with required standards of accuracy, coherence, order and so forth. Effective teaching depends on providing these opportunities. In achieving this, the following general principles may be helpful.

Choosing materials whose content is worthwhile

Both the content of materials used and the tasks set for performance by the pupils need to be worthy in themselves of the attention of able young 16–19-year-olds, quite apart from their supposed value as instruments of language acquisition. Language teachers in the sixth form are, like their colleagues in other subjects, under an obligation to promote the general intellectual development of their pupils, their understanding of themselves and of society, of the major issues of the day and of more lasting concern, of differing opinions and alternative perspectives. These need to be exemplified and debated in the various materials placed before students at this stage. In addition, communicative skill may be more effectively learned if the language is being used by the pupil to say something that he or she actually wants to say, whether this be in passing on information, expressing a passionately held conviction or expounding a genuinely held point of view.

Exploiting potential for individual work

It is important at this stage to exploit the potential of students for independent work outside of contact time. It is essential to foster the capacity for self-directed and unsupervised work as a preparation for either responsible employment or higher education. The skilful utilisation of private study time also allows for a great deal more to be achieved. The usual seven or eight periods a week available for an A-level subject would be an extremely meagre and fragmented allowance of time in which to learn all that has to be learned. It is important not to overburden one's pupils and prevent them from enjoying a full and rounded social and family life, but the good management of private study time may enable learning time in class to be doubled or trebled. Many conscientious students will, in any case, spend much time brooding over their work. It is therefore desirable to provide well-structured and efficient learning tasks rather than leaving them to slog away in depressing and unproductive toil.

This may entail giving some thought to the management and monitoring of private study. It is no longer possible to simply set the next passage in the book for translation over the weekend or to announce an essay title off the top of one's head. Tasks and materials need to be consciously identified in advance and may need some adaptation. Work set well in advance is likely to receive more attention than if no room is left for manœuvre or negotiation in the event of a clash with other demands. Effective private study necessarily entails the provision of dictionaries, reference books and other materials under good access conditions if not issued individually. Recorded as well as printed materials may be used for private study, but even though many students nowadays possess private cassette recorders it is also desirable to provide a number of listening positions in the library or similar place. The setting of joint assignments or work to be done in pairs has the virtue of developing the habits of cooperation and professional consultation and the discussion of what is to be written down or said in class is itself a learning experience. Where reading or learning is set for private study this needs to be checked either formally or informally on a regular basis, otherwise it may come to be squeezed out of the students' busy schedule by the pressure of more urgent demands.

Organising work in substantial units

Work needs to be organised in identifiable topic-units extending over a fortnight or more. This not only avoids the 'My God, what shall I give them next lesson?' syndrome but is satisfying to the students who have the feeling of getting their teeth into something substantial. Materials provided in the most widely used sixth-form courses rarely provide sufficient variety for this purpose and may need to be supplemented from other sources. Sustained attention to a particular topic using a variety of modes and registers ensures that certain ideas and issues, as well as certain linguistic items will recur, be reinforced and may therefore stand a chance of becoming part of pupils' active intellectual and linguistic stock. By contrast, new language encountered in a one-off piece of material on a given topic may be forgotten as soon as the bell goes, especially if no follow-up task is set. Ideally, students need to be set a culminating piece of written work or oral presentation to be completed by the end of the period during which work on the topic is covered. In this way they are mentally set to observe and note material in the course of other work on the topic area which may be incorporated in the final assignment. If such topics can arise from background books or even literary works being studied, so much the better. To provide experience of an appropriate range of modes and registers, however, it will need to be supplemented from a number of other sources.

Activities during the period in which the topic is being studied must ensure that all four language skills are kept in play, and may usefully include some of the following:

1. Reading a fairly lengthy text for information or gist. This may conveniently be done out of contact time with open-ended guide questions (in the language) or some simple focusing task to provide for semi-prepared discussion in class. Alternatively, gist comprehension work may be set as a group task in contact time, it being understood, of course, that the discussion of guide quesions is to be carried out in the language.

2. Intensive study of a more difficult, idiomatically rich or stylistically interesting passage. This is essentially a teacher-led activity in which the attention of the class is drawn to unfamiliar words or other points by means of such devices as question and answer aimed at prompting use of the word or idiom at issue.

3. The above activities using printed text may be paralleled using recorded material, and may be reinforced by such relatively more formal activities as summary, transcription, retranslation and gapped exercises. The full audio-active-comparative language laboratory (i.e. with independent recorders in each booth) continues to provide ideal conditions for extended listening. Sixth-form language broadcasts are ideal for this purpose, especially when backed up with worksheets or note-taking tasks. It is sometimes suggested that similar conditions can be achieved by the use of relatively cheap play-back cassette recorders. The language laboratory, however, also provides for recorded and oral summary or other responses to what is heard, as well as for monitoring by the teacher.

At the beginning of the period when a particular topic is being studied it is obviously desirable that receptive, text-based or recording-based activities should predominate. One is best placed to use the language relating to a particular topic area with a degree of fluency after having first heard it being used by others. The content of texts and recordings used will also serve to stimulate the student's own thoughts and responses to the topic. As the period of study proceeds, however, there will be a natural move towards more active and creative uses of the language. These may include oral summary and discussion of passages and recordings read or heard, the group preparation of formal or informal debates and the class discussion, with appropriate teacher guidance and inputs, of related topics. They may also include class discussion, preparation and guidance for the final presentation or piece of written work. If this is to be at all profitable such guidance and support needs to be fairly intensive at the start of the sixth-form course and may include the discussion of structure and layout, an indication of the range of content and argument to be included, and a reminder as to where these may be found in work previously studied. It may also include the joint drafting of key passages and collective discussion and embellishment of individual first efforts. Needless to say, progress through the sixth form will naturally be accompanied by a gradual weaning off from this early and highly necessary degree of support, to the point where written work or oral presentation can be prepared for without specific guidance. For the ability to produce work independently in the language is the required objective whether the student will end his or her language studies at the end of the sixth, or continue with them in higher or further education.

TEACHING STUDENTS TO RESPOND TO LITERARY WORKS

Clearly it is a highly efficient procedure as far as possible to integrate work on books studied as literature or as part of a background studies element with other language work. In the case of literature, however, especially where questions will eventually have to be answered in English, teachers will also be aware of a number of objectives which cannot be regarded purely linguistic in the same way as other work on textual or recorded material. It cannot be sufficiently stressed, however, that far from standing in stark contrast to language, literature is simply one particularly sophisticated form of linguistic communication. In a sense, therefore, the reading of a work of literature is a particular kind of reading comprehension in which, however, the full import of the message goes far beyond the literal meaning of the words on the page. In principle, what the author is attempting to say may be understood from the text with, perhaps, the addition of a small amount of information about the personal and cultural context in which the work was written. The task is to elicit an understanding of the work, or significant parts of it, from the class. This has little to do with a number of unproductive teaching approaches still used in many sixth forms. These include translation of the text in class, either by the students, or as often as not, by the teacher, the giving of notes on details of the author's life, times, ideas and beliefs, whether or not these are of strict relevance to the particular text, the marking of important quotes to be learned and, above all, desultory and unstructured line-by-line comment on the text by the teacher. These processes may or may not be accompanied by a general injunction to 'prepare' the text in advance.

Such procedures are bound to be ineffectual both in promoting the skill of understanding literary works and, for that matter, of demonstrating such an understanding by writing essays or commentaries in an examination. Literal understanding of the words of the text may in no sense be equivalent to a grasp of the author's meaning.

In most of these procedures the student is more or less entirely passive, whereas skills can only be learnt by active participation in conjunction with encouragement and correction. Teachers' notes often cannot be interpreted or applied in coming to an understanding of the particular work. Where these are general critical remarks they are often simply accepted wholesale as if they were facts like the content of geography or physics. At best they tend to lead the student to look for examples of a certain feature of the author's work which has been mentioned by the teacher, rather than responding to the particular work being studied.

Desultory line-by-line commentary does not lead to a coherent grasp of the work and does not build students' confidence in their ability to respond to the text for themselves. On the contrary, it engenders the view that literature is hard and boring and that one must have a good deal of previous knowledge, not to say second sight into what will be regarded as a suitable comment, before one can expect to be any good at it. The reluctance of many language teachers to teach modern texts which they have not themselves studied at university, on the grounds that they have 'no information' about them, ultimately results from their having experienced such passive teaching methods themselves.

If literature is to be taught effectively, pupils must at least be credited with the ability to read most of the text in their own time. This may need to be structured, guided and monitored very carefully in the early stages. Specific reading assignments need to be set, not in terms of 25 pages per week, but in significant units, acts, scenes, chapters, etc. so that the work is seen to be composed of significant parts rather than as an endless flow of undifferentiated material.

Understanding needs to be supported by means of guide questions which, by implication, draw attention to the significant issues raised by the passage read. Questions designed for this purpose may have the appearance of being simple and straightforward, while actually drawing attention to key issues in the work, or important literary features. In setting students to read the account of Paneloux's first sermon in Camus's *La Peste* one might ask:

'Why does Paneloux think the plague has broken out at Oran?'
'Does this seem to be a satisfactory explanation of evil in the world? Would it be an appropriate response to any of the recent natural disasters we have experienced?'
'What sort of person do you think Paneloux is?'
'What is the weather like while he is preaching? Has Camus referred to the weather in any other parts of the book?'

This is no more than gist comprehension, yet the task of answering these questions plus some later discussion of the answers in class will be more helpful – both from the point of view of students' literary understanding and from that of answering essay questions – than several lessons spent in translating the chapter or writing notes on the philosophy of Existentialism or the biography of its originators. It will also prove more enjoyable to students and teachers alike. If, in the course of discussion, it becomes clear that a key sentence has been completely misunderstood one may then return to it and even have it translated, to be on the safe side. Close study and questioning, however, will normally make this unnecessary. As the course proceeds, guide questions will become increasingly open-ended:

'What is this chapter about?'
'Why has the author put it in?'
'What do you think we ought to comment on?'

Pupils who are able to respond satisfactorily to questions of this nature are autonomous and now in a position to study works of literature without the aid of a schoolteacher.

The purpose of the guide questions has been to encourage students to look closely at the text and to articulate their response to it. Where this is misguided, it is always possible to send pupils back to the text itself for reconsideration, rather than rely on the authority of some critical work. This, in itself, is valuable preparation for the writing of essay-type answers.

The writing of essays themselves, however, may require some further guidance. It is important that essay-type questions should be set well in advance so that pupils have a chance to mull over what is required in the course of reading the text and discussing it in class and raise any queries or anxieties they may have. In the early stages passages of particular relevance to the questions set may need to be indicated, or specifically referred to in discussion. To begin with it is also helpful actually to plan the structure of an essay together in class before pupils attempt to write it. Surprisingly, perhaps, this does not result in a batch of identical essays, for pupils will respond to the same passage or express the same point differently. Such guidance will, however, prevent opportunities being lost through failure to focus on important parts of the book, and provide a model of sensible planning for pupils to follow on future occasions.

Where it is decided to use the foreign language for discussing the text, whether or not answers in the examination have to be written in the foreign language, the process is not substantially different. By setting pupils to prepare their own comments on the work one makes good use of independent study time and ensures that students will be active and productive, as well as reading carefully for comprehension of the text as a whole, rather than for points of detail. As when guide questions are given and answered in the mother tongue it is important to set fairly open-ended questions, and discourage the practice of reading out written answers. This defeats one of the objects of the exercise which is to allow all members of the class to acquire practice in expressing serious ideas orally in the language, and to make those ideas their own through the process of discussion.

Whether the teaching medium is the mother tongue or the foreign language many of the teacher inputs are essentially the same, namely, the asking of probing questions, sending pupils back to the text to check and modify statements, as well as the discussion-management tasks of controlling the exuberant and protecting and encouraging the timid. In addition, when the foreign language is being used the teacher will have an additional responsibility for promoting the language development of his pupils. How far the teacher should intervene to correct actual linguistic errors will be a matter of judgement. Repeated errors certainly need to be corrected at a convenient point and there is a need to guard against the habit of pidgin or incoherent speech. Here a request for clarification may be more effective than actual correction by providing the student with an opportunity for second and more careful thoughts about what he has to say.

It is a further important requirement that the teacher should be ready and able to help out when a pupil is struggling to say something but is short of a particular word or expression. This is a somewhat delicate art, for the task is to enable students to say what *they* want to say, not to say it for them, and certainly not to say something cleverer and more sophisticated instead. For that is precisely to destroy the students' burgeoning confidence in their ability to use the language to express important and serious ideas for themselves. Sometimes a probing question containing the item that the student needs will be helpful. One may, of course, also supply the item more explicitly: 'L' expression que vous cherchez, c'est "la confiance en soi!" Alors, Hugo manque de . . . Allez, c'est bien ce que vous dites là.' Alternatively, one may ask another member of the group to help out, but if this is done, one needs immediately to bring the discussion back to the original student, so that he does not become discouraged, or feel that he has lost the floor through ineptness.

The criterion of a successful lesson of this kind is not the over-all amount of true things about the book that are said and written down, but the number of things, true or false, that are said by the students. A useful monitoring device in this regard is to ask a student to keep a tally of the number of contributions made to the discussion by the teacher, and other members of the group, with contributions of more than one sentence counting double. Informal observation by the present writer suggests that, in a successful lesson, the tally of the teacher will be slightly less than that of all the students combined. More importantly, however, a distinction is to be drawn between various utterances by the teacher. That which concerns us most is the distinction between those contributions that are probing questions or expressions of encouragement which stimulate or prolong comments from students, and those which purport to make auth-oritative statements, to which no response is necessary or even possible. In the successful lesson, the number of these latter 'contributions' by the teacher will be minimal, except where they are required to clarify or summarise what has been said. Normally, they will tend to cluster towards the end of a session after students have had the fullest opportunity to explore their own thoughts.

When the foreign language is being used, it is even more important than with the mother tongue that formal written work should be preceded by careful guidance and class discussion, with a progressive weaning off towards independence as the course progresses. In particular, the writing of rough drafts to be read out and discussed by the class before the final version is submitted is a very profitable teaching procedure, much appreci-ated by students at this level.

DEVELOPING BACKGROUND READING

There is now widespread agreement among many language teachers that as an alternative to literary studies A-level students should follow an assessed programme of wider reading or back-ground studies. It is also all but universally agreed that such a programme should be assessed by means of answers or essays written in the foreign language. It is assumed that this will encourage the use of the foreign language as the medium of teaching and learning.

Programmes may comprise a study of particular aspects of the country whose language is being studied, or of its culture. Though books will no doubt provide the principal source of information for many students, there is certainly provision for the study of other media such as the press, TV and radio broad-casting. Where schools or pupils have particular connections with a particular region in the foreign country, it may also be possible to offer assessment work based on direct investi-gation and enquiry carried out in the area concerned (AEB 1986: 8). Regrettably, some of the books suggested by some boards for background study may be in English. Hopefully, the proportion of such works will decrease as time progresses and the members of examining boards become more familiar with works in the foreign language.

As an alternative to topics specifically related to the foreign country, students may be encouraged to study a contemporary issue of more universal application, as treated by authors writing in the language being studied. The works in question may include both fiction and non-fiction, but where literary works are included, it is clearly specified that they are to be read for content and interest, not for literary comment. Broadly, two modes of assessing the reading programme or background studies have emerged. Students may be required to write fairly extended answers in the language under traditional examination con-ditions. The AEB (1985: 18) for example, requires two essays of 350 words on two different topics. More radical is the Joint Matriculation Board (JMB) option of writing three course-work essays totalling some 3,000 words. Unfortunately this innovation has encountered some opposition from teachers because of the burden of supervision and assessment involved (JMB 1986: 3–4), but may nevertheless continue to be followed in some schools and colleges. In the assessment of answers or essays written in the language, some marks are awarded for linguistic accuracy. The majority, however, are allocated to content and such qual-ities as the ability to convey ideas and information in a clear, coherent and well-organised fashion in the language.

It has to be said that although there is general agreement that such developments are highly desirable, there has been relatively little public discussion within the language-teaching profession as to how they are to be handled pedagogically. Good work is certainly being done in many institutions. Background studies have been offered as an alternative to literature for some time, and the JMB proposals have been carefully piloted.

Many of the principles set out in the previous section with regard to the teaching of literature will certainly also apply in work of this kind. Whether background knowledge and the reading programme are studied on a group basis, or in the form of individual projects, the careful management and monitoring of individual reading and, in the case of course-work, individual written work is essential. Though students may be encouraged to choose their reading independently, they need opportunities for discussing this with their teacher to ensure that it is appropriate in terms of volume, level and relevance. Whatever hard-bitten members of the profession may think, there is a danger that many anxious and well-meaning students will take on too ambitious a programme or fall into the trap of annotating in too much detail. Where course-work projects are undertaken on an individual basis, the advising and guidance of students may require particular skills, as was often stressed in the use of European Studies projects at a more elementary stage (Wringe 1976: 100–8). Not least among these is the ability to diagnose where a particular student's interest lies or to transform a student's unduly general or unduly narrow proposal into an undertaking of appropriate amplitude. In the case of individual projects the clear identification of adequate sources is essential. Normally, this will entail that they are immediately and readily available in the school itself, so that a policy of building up appropriate departmental and library resources is an essential prerequisite of effective work in this area.

As with the study of literary works using the foreign language, prime teaching procedures are preparation, on the basis of guided reading for class discussion and presentation, followed by appropriately handled discussion and presentation themselves. Equally valuable are group discussion and elaboration of essay and study plans and the discussion of drafts prior to completing final versions for handing in.

Possibly, in the case of factual topics, it may be felt appropriate for the teacher to make some formal input in the language. He may even encourage pupils to make notes and give some guidance as to how this should be done. If this procedure is used at all, however, it should be severely limited to aspects of a topic on which the teacher may be supposed to have special knowledge and upon which no accessible and adequately comprehensive source can be identified.

At this level as elsewhere in education, discussion and cooperative work between students, or between students and teacher, are highly effective learning procedures. Where work is to be handed in for assessment under the JMB course-work option, however, there must be no specific correction of drafts by the teacher and cooperation between students must stop short at the point at which the actual piece of written work submitted ceases to be the unaided work of the individual candidate.

REVIEW AND ENHANCEMENT

1. If you have not already done so, spend some time discussing students' other subjects, interests and career aspirations with them.
   (a) Identify any committed linguists and note the proportion of these to those who see the language as a secondary skill supporting a main interest.
   (b) Review projected material for the course. If necessary, identify supplementary material in the light of students' other interests as well as stylistically interesting texts, or texts whose content is of particular interest to committed linguists.
2. Review projected language work for the term.
   (a) Divide into an appropriate number of major topics. Provisionally identify culminating assignments and set provisional dates for handing in.
   (b) Plan a topic in detail, taking account of the distribution of lesson times and facilities available on each occasion. In particular, identify all materials and private study tasks in advance. Make a provisional estimate of time required for private study tasks envisaged and expand or reduce accordingly.
   (c) Build in time for class discussion of the culminating assignment and parts of students' initial drafts.
   (d) Record a lesson in which a substantial piece of material or a prepared theme is discussed in the foreign language. Attempt to quantify your own and students' contributions. Consider ways in which the latter might have been increased by means of more careful guidance in preparation or more probing or open-ended questions. Note any occasions on which you yourself said things that could have been elicited from students. Note the distribution of students' contributions. If necessary consider how some students could have been encouraged to contribute more, or how others could have been prevented from dominating the discussion.
3. Consider a literary text to be studied in the near future.
   (a) Divide into major reading assignments with provisional dates.
   (b) Provisionally identify possible written assignments or other forms of student presentation.

(c) Take a substantial section of the text and identify major themes or central ideas. Devise a short list of questions of an appropriate level, whose answers depend on central themes or ideas being recognised. Identify page and line references of parts of the text which will be of particular help in answering the questions set.

(d) Set the section of the text to be read with guide questions and references to key parts of the text. Use questions as a basis for class discussion, attempting to keep your own contributions to a minimum except where necessary to supply information or correct obvious misapprehensions.

4. Review procedures and materials for background reading.

(a) Note topics chosen for study during the preceding two years. Review available materials for each and supplement where necessary.

(b) Review procedures for guiding pupils in their initial choice of topics. Consider whether appropriate general guidance is given before students make their initial choice, and whether sufficient time is set aside for individual or group discussion of topics. Consider whether pupils are required to be sufficiently specific in their plans at a sufficiently early point. Plan to amend practice as necessary in the light of the above.

(c) Review procedures for comment and guidance. Ensure that these allow maximum interaction and discussion between students (consistently with fair practice in relation to the examination).

(d) Identify ways of increasing oral discussion in the language of all assignments before students write their final draft.

FURTHER READING

Bird E 1981 'Sixth form language work', in D G Smith (ed.) *Teaching Languages in Today's Schools.* Centre for Information on Language Teaching and Research, London, pp 103–14

Corless F 1978 'A new look at literary studies in the sixth form modern language course', *Audio Visual Language Journal*, **16** (3), 161–70

Schools Council 1970 *Working Paper No. 28: New Patterns in Sixth Form Modern Language Studies.* Evans/Methuen, London

Smith D G 1981 'Sixth form 'A' level literature' in D G Smith, *Teaching Languages in Today's Schools.* Centre for Information on Language Teaching and Research, London, pp 115–26

As with the syllabus for the GCSE, those for the revised A-level examinations offered by the various boards are, in the main, full and informative in explaining their requirements and rationale.

CHAPTER 9

Using aids and technology

The title of this chapter may be interpreted fairly broadly to refer to the use of:

1. Traditional teaching aids such as pictures, posters, flash-cards, diagrams and, of course, the blackboard and chalk or its modern equivalents.
2. Established language-teaching technology such as the overhead projector, audio and video recorders, projectors, copiers and the language laboratory.
3. Information technology, notably the micro-computer.

It will be unnecessary to detail the advantages of items in the first two categories. This has been done many times (e.g. Smalley and Morris 1985: 93–133) and forms part of the common stock-in-trade of the language-teaching profession. There is equally little need to make obvious points about the need for legible hand-outs or audible recordings, or to stress the importance of ensuring that images projected on screens are properly focused and visible in prevailing lighting conditions, that equipment is kept in good repair and so on. Clearly there can be no effective use of teaching aids without attention to these elementary matters.

More useful purpose will be served by pointing to a number of general principles governing the use and management of teaching aids, against which the policies and practices of both departments and individual teachers may be assessed.

THE TEACHING AID AS STIMULUS

In contrast perhaps to some other subjects, the purpose of an aid or piece of material in the language lesson is often not to convey subject content as much as to provide stimulus, something for the class to write or talk about in language. This applies obviously enough to the set of flash-cards of items sold in the supermarket or the family tree gradually built up on the OHP. It may, however, be equally true of the photocopied text, recorded dialogue or adventure-game programme used on the micro-computer.

In deciding whether or not to use a particular aid or piece of technology the essential question to ask is not 'What is the content of the material being used?' but 'What language activity will it enable to take place?'

ECONOMY IN THE USE OF TEACHING AIDS

It is a common-sense principle that teaching aids and technology should not be used to achieve purposes that can as well be achieved by simpler means. A computer program to teach the German adjectival endings, for example, might quite properly be criticised if it amounted to no more than a gap-filling exercise that could as well have been printed in a book or written on the blackboard, and many things can as easily be written on the blackboard as projected on the OHP. If setting up the projector seriously cuts into lesson time, or tension produced by the complexities of the language laboratory console makes the teacher insensitive to the boredom or misunderstandings of the class, then projector and laboratory are best dispensed with. Some pieces of language are best taught by means of the spoken or written word alone, uncluttered by technological paraphernalia.

The principle that teaching aids and technology should not be used beyond necessity should not, however, be interpreted too austerely for, besides being a mask for complacency, this may cause us to overlook the motivating effect of novelty and slickness of presentation. If the teacher's building up of a situation by means of successive overlays on the OHP is ingenious or manages to create surprise or amusement, the content of the lesson may be remembered more readily and pupils may come to the next lesson in a more heightened mood of expectancy.

Ideally, however, teaching aids and technology should not depend for their value on their motivating effect alone but either:

(a) enable things to be done that could otherwise not be done at all; or
(b) enable some things that language teachers have always done to be done more efficiently or more easily.

Instances of the first will leap readily to mind. When many existing language teachers began their careers the possibility of bringing authentic foreign voices or even a variety of authentic printed materials into the classroom did not exist. Such tape recorders as there were 20 years ago were bulky, intimidating and unreliable, while the written materials that could be placed before the class were limited to those in the textbook or capable of being written in biro on a Banda master, or typed on a wax-covered Gestetner sheet.

The use of video rather than audio recordings for listening comprehension may seem an unnecessary, and possibly even cumbersome, refinement. The video, however, transmits to the pupil a mass of information, largely tacit, about the foreign country and its people, about the experience of being in the country and hearing and seeing the language spoken, in a way not equalled by the audio medium.

The principle of using technology to achieve something that could not have been seriously attempted before must nevertheless be treated with caution. In the 1960s the tape recorder and the language laboratory were seized upon as a means of orchestrating multiple repetition with a degree of persistence and discipline not previously possible. Audio-lingual and audio-visual methods took over the whole of the language-teaching process for a brief period, with results that were far from happy. The lesson to be drawn is that simply because something new *can* be done with the aid of new technology this is not to say that it *must* be done, and certainly not that it must be done all the time.

Two, in principle, admirable pieces of technology seem currently to run particular risk of abuse in this way. These are the photocopier which makes possible the production, among other things, of multiple worksheets, and the OHP.

The worksheet is a time-honoured and perfectly valid educational device, making possible individual work with a degree of flexibility not possible with the use of the textbook alone. Being expendable and therefore able to be written on, it enables individual work, especially in the receptive skills, to be done by pupils for whom the production of any extensive piece of writing is too difficult a task.

The danger, however, is that the worksheet provides an all too easy way of 'giving a class something to get on with', thus cutting down interaction both between pupil and pupil and pupil and teacher. This is especially true with 'good' worksheets where the instructions are clear and explicit and require little class discussion or elaboration.

It is therefore desirable to monitor and limit one's use of worksheets, regarding with particular suspicion those which require little discussion or preparation or involve even the weakest members of the class in little real difficulty. Where worksheets can be completed cooperatively, however, this may turn a clerkly penance into a genuine learning experience.

The OHP is a boon to language teachers for many reasons. Its ability to be switched on or off at a moment's notice, or to allow material to be progressively built up or revealed by the use of overlays enables an element of suspense and surprise to be maintained, and information given at the psychological moment and unobtrusively withdrawn when no longer needed. Diagrams, texts, tables and other dense information can also be temporarily shown without the need for laborious writing on the blackboard, or the clutter of printed sheets. Vocabulary and exemplary sentences can be written down and projected as they emerge in the course of loosely structured oral work without too obviously interrupting the flow of interaction. Informal experimentation by the present writer suggests that, in question-and-answer work using the OHP, the number of interactions is increased by about one-third compared with similar work using the blackboard. The proportion of new material actually written up is also substantially increased.

As with the use of worksheets, however, there are caveats to be observed. In certain respects the OHP is more suitable to the lecture-room than the classroom. Like many audio-visual aids it focuses attention upon the teacher and his performance rather than on the activity of the pupil. The slight hum of the fan which no model yet appears to have eliminated, encourages the teacher to speak firmly and emphatically in order to avoid distraction, and may increase one's irritation and impatience as pupils grope for a reply or speak softly or hesitantly when they are unsure of themselves. There is in consequence a danger that the teacher will hesitate to encourage contributions from the class while prepared transparencies serve to back up and illustrate what the teacher has set out to say rather than responding flexibly to pupils' contributions.

No general condemnation of either worksheets or the OHP is intended. Quite the contrary. The point is simply that one should monitor one's enthusiasm for the use of any particular aid or device. All such devices necessarily influence one's teaching style in directions which are particularly consonant with their use. This may be harmless or even advantageous, but one needs to remain alert to the overall effect on the pupils' activity and experience.

WHICH MEDIUM?

In addition to enabling things to be done which could not be done before, technology may also enable some time-honoured language-teaching activities to be undertaken more efficiently by removing non-productive drudgery and enabling the same pedagogic task to be presented more briskly or more memorably. The diversity of available media necessarily imposes a burden of choice upon the teacher. Having decided what material he is to use he must also decide how best it may be presented.

A photocopied text or exercise may be better than one written on the blackboard because the teacher is free to attend to the pupils as they begin to study it, to answer their questions or simply note how easily it is understood. But against this, a precopied exercise cannot easily be modified in the light of the way the lesson has gone.

Words and structures required in the narration of a particular kind of incident may be presented by means of a printed text, or through discussion of a recorded narrative, or series of pictures. The first ensures that the pupils see the written word and requires less to be put on the board or OHP. Using a recording provides practice in aural comprehension, whereas the use of pictures alone is demanding in terms of oral production, but enables the teacher to adapt his interpretation to the ability and mood of his class.

A menu may be written on the board, given on a hand-out or projected with the OHP. The first economises on out-of-class preparation time. The last is efficient in class, but may be time-consuming to organise and unsuitable if the material has to be available for a large part of the lesson, or kept permanently by the pupils!

There will rarely be one obvious answer to the question of which medium should be used. For teaching to be maximally effective, however, it is essential that the choice should be made after critical consideration of the options available, in relation to one's overall aims and the needs of particular groups, rather than as a result of inertia or fleeting predilection for a particular mode of presentation.

THE MANAGEMENT OF TEACHING AIDS

If teachers are to make frequent and appropriate use of teaching aids and technology in the light of pedagogic needs they must not be deterred by difficulties in locating or obtaining the item they have decided to use, or by the unpredictability of its availability. Whatever may be maintained to the contrary, effective teaching is planned teaching, not a series of inspired performances off the top of one's head because the OHP one had intended to use was inextricably wedged beneath a mass of brooms and PE kit, or the school micro was required by the head of geography who regards it as his personal possession.

The effective use of equipment requires convenient storage and proper management, for no piece of equipment is as ineffective as that which occupies valuable space but is rarely used. In principle there are three main strategies for the storage and steward-ship of equipment.

1. Permanent location in teaching rooms

Obviously it would be ideal if all language-teaching rooms contained as standard an OHP, tape recorder, slide/filmstrip projector and screen together with such tapes, slides, filmstrips textbooks and other course materials as were required by classes using those rooms. As an alternative to this a suite of adjacent rooms may be regularly used for language classes with items of equipment kept in various of those rooms and removed only by special arrangement. Provided classes are not always timetabled for the same one of the language rooms one can then at least rely on having, say, the laboratory on Monday, an OHP on Wednesday and the slide projector for the double period on Thursday. Though this may seem somewhat inflexible it at least minimises the need to carry equipment from place to place with the risks or loss, breakage and simple forgetfulness this entails, and one can plan one's work around what one knows one will have at one's disposal. With bulky or immovable items of equipment this may be the only possible strategy.

2. Individual responsibility for particular items

This is the obvious strategy for cassette tape recorders which must be regarded as constantly in use by all teachers. Modern syllabuses cannot properly be taught unless teachers can regularly let their pupils hear recorded material. Sharing arrangements may sometimes be necessary but are less than ideal. If the recorder is only available, say, twice a week all one's listening activities must be crowded into those periods, however inappropriate that may be in the sequencing of one's work. If a recorder is shared between two or more individuals on an informal basis it will tend to be under-used by the junior or less assertive individual. If recorders are centrally stored and few in number, availability cannot be counted on and lesson plans will often need to be changed at short notice.

Often, less frequently used items may also be entrusted to the safe keeping of particular colleagues. That way at least one knows how to locate a piece of equipment, and with whom to negotiate for its use even if the feeling that 'the OHP belongs to Mr Brown' may inhibit other members of the department from using it as often as might be desirable.

3. Central storage

This is the most economical and convenient arrangement in large institutions with ancillary staff. These maintain equipment in good order, keep track of it when it is taken out and may even arrange for it to be transported to and from the room where it is needed.

When ancillary staff are not available to manage aids and equipment on a school basis, central storage of equipment at a departmental level may often be a convenient arrangement, particularly where rooms regularly used for language teaching are close together and there is a central store accessible from most of them. If this arrangement is to be satisfactory someone in the department needs to be charged with the general oversight of equipment and materials, both to arrange for repairs and replacements when necessary and to establish working procedures and draw attention to them when they are not followed. In a small department in which informal communications are good such procedures need not be formalised, but both efficiency and good relations require colleagues to be meticulous about such matters as returning items immediately after use, booking out so that missing items can quickly be traced, respecting advance reservations and reporting faults and deficiencies. The inconvenience and frustration caused by failure to observe such courtesies is bound to disturb and discourage the habit of automatically making use of whatever piece of equipment seems most suitable for a given purpose, and many lessons will be less than optimally effective in consequence.

TEACHER-MADE AIDS AND RECORDINGS

During initial training and on the occasion of visits by inspectors and advisers the liberal use of teacher-made aids and materials is likely to come in for high praise as the sign of both a creative approach and personal commitment. It would certainly be perverse to discourage teachers who have the flair and inclination to produce imaginative materials of their own. But, as in all things, effectiveness is a function of time and effort spent (and therefore taken away from other activities) as measured against output in terms of pupil learning. It may be thought that if a teacher creates his own materials in his leisure time this is, from the school's point of view, 'all profit'. But the teacher who works for excessively long hours is not likely to prove effective in the long run.

The alternative to creating all one's own materials is not traditional textbook teaching but sensible adaptation in which an available course is used with a degree of independence. Some audio-visual units may serve as models for communicative dialogues or as material for listening comprehension. Pictures for traditional 150-word composition may be cut up and the story reconstituted in group discussion. Older passages intended to be translated round the class may be skimmed and scanned for reading comprehension, or serve as the basis for narrative reports and letters. Such adaptive use of professionally prepared if, now, somewhat old-fashioned materials may prove more effective and no less challenging than what sometimes amounts to the self-indulgence of creating substantial amounts of one's own material *de novo*.

When one does use one's own materials, it is important that they should not need to be remade every time they are required. Where it does not detract from their authenticity it obviously makes sense for pictorial aids not to be language specific. A *boulangerie* is unmistakably French and may as well have the name of Jacques Durand over the shop front, but locomotives, swimming-pools and baskets of fruit may look rather similar in many countries and the same sketch or diagram may be used for teaching more than one language. Materials that are to be used over and over again may merit a little more care in the making. Pictures may be worth drawing on card and covering with adhesive film, for example. It is always worth running off extra copies of texts and worksheets, or at least carefully preserving the master. Systematic storage is a must even if the thought that one will not be needing a particular piece of material again for another year may act as a disincentive in a busy week. Some writers advocate the sharing of materials. This, however, needs careful management, and the support of all members of the department. Keener members may feel less than gratified to find that their carefully made and generously contributed materials have been lost or mangled by less considerate colleagues.

In language departments, teacher-made materials naturally include recorded tapes. Few schools now expect the soundproof and acoustically designed recording studios often demanded in the 1960s. It is, however, often possible to adapt a small room which may double as a departmental store or small tutorial room. The essential requirements are access during free periods, convenient electrical sockets, a working surface, seats and suitable lighting. Basic equipment would ideally comprise a cassette recorder or better, radio-cassette recorder, for making off-air recordings, a good-quality microphone, tape copying or editing facilities (linked recorders or twin cassette machine) and, most importantly, an ample supply of clean C 60 cassettes which are explicitly defined as consumable materials. If money can be found for an automatic time-switch for making off-air recordings overnight and, maybe, a bulk eraser, so much the better.

Such a list is not extensive and does not include luxurious or prestige items. Provision of the above facility would greatly enhance a school's ability to meet the requirement to provide access to an adequate quantity and variety of authentic spoken language and the overall cost cannot be considered great.

The content of school-made tapes may derive from various sources. The pirating of recorded material not purchased by the school is, of course, illegal. The making of several copies for use within the same institution, however, appears to be generally regarded as acceptable. Recordings of interviews and role-plays with foreign assistants (where available), staff and pupils from one's exchange school and other contacts in the foreign country are invaluable as, of course, are BBC and ITV language programmes.

Little need be said about the desirability of sensible labelling, orderly storage of tapes or the avoidance of coercive or cumbersome cataloguing procedures. Particularly desirable is an annual clearing out of tapes that are no longer required. As a rule of thumb anything that has not been used for, say, two years is probably best erased unless there are good reasons for doing otherwise.

REHABILITATING THE LANGUAGE LABORATORY

The language laboratory is a much-neglected and much-maligned facility. No doubt it awaits a sudden technological leap forward as a result of computerisation. One reason for the disfavour into which it has fallen is the isolating effect of sitting in an enclosed booth and, even when there are no dividing panels, the wearing of earphones. This inhibits all group communication and group learning. Interaction is typically between the teacher and one pupil so that, in a period of 30 minutes with a class of 30, contact time, even when the teacher monitors assiduously throughout, amounts on average to less than one minute per pupil. For the remainder of the time the pupil is necessarily 'on his own', without responsive feedback or encouragement from either teacher or classmates.

This is compounded by the tedious and repetitive activities which have typically been carried out in the laboratory as the result of a sterile and, as it now appears, misguided language learning theory (see Wringe 1976: 11–13).

The full audio-active-comparative laboratory with independently controlled machines in each booth, however, is ideally suited for many valuable and more varied activities, including listening comprehension in a situation in which the listener can to some degree control the rate of input. In the laboratory the pupil can pause the tape in order to process what he has heard, before proceeding to the next section, or listen several times to key passages.

In the field of aural comprehension, in which some pupils progress very quickly indeed, it is valuable for pupils to work at their own pace rather than be tediously held back or hurried and hassled along at the average pace of the class. Much comprehension work is ideally carried out on the library basis with individuals or groups being given different material, or encouraged to complete more material of increasing difficulty according to ability.

Role-play of the kind where the foreign speaker's responses are of a highly predictable kind may also be very economically and effectively practised in the language laboratory.

Even much-criticised drill exercises can be adapted along communicative lines. There is little place for those which were mere grammatical transformations of a collection of disparate sentences. But if cue and response can be made to resemble a snatch of authentic dialogue appropriate to whatever area of language is being studied, the exercises may be quite valid, for example:

Cue: Des pommes peut-être?
Response: Oui, je voudrais un kilo de pommes, s'il vous plaît, Monsieur.
Cue: Des tomates, peut-être?
Response: Oui, je voudrais un kilo de tomates s'il vous plaît, Monsieur.
Cue: Des oranges . . . etc.

The language laboratory may also be used in an extended programme containing various activities. This works particularly well with older, perhaps slightly disaffected pupils who may welcome the chance of working independently. A programme in which pupils are guided by a worksheet might include some of the following:

(a) A dialogue for listening comprehension.
(b) Related role-play or communicative drills.
(c) A *short* piece of repetition choosing a key part of the listening comprehension material.
(d) Transcribing a short passage, to be self-marked from a key provided.
(e) An opportunity for oral composition such as summarising or reporting what was said in the passage for aural comprehension.
(f) Writing a brief note arising from the above activities.

There is no reason why such a programme should not be worked through in pairs, with two pupils plugged into each booth. This overcomes both the problem of isolation and that of the 16-booth laboratory, where these continue to exist.

Regarding the type of language laboratory installation, some authorities have, as an economy measure, installed so-called audio-active systems, either in all booths or in some of them. In audio-active booths pupils do not have individual recorders under their control but simply hear the output of a central recorder in the console. Individual monitoring is possible and pupils' voices are fed back into the headset via a microphone, supposedly so that they can judge the quality of their own utterances. The value of such installations is frankly dubious if, indeed, their effect on teaching methods is not positively pernicious.

If it is thought that there is benefit in having pupils respond to a central recording not under their individual control, this can be more cheaply done with a set of simple output sockets and earphones (an 'audio-passive' system) or, for that matter, in unison around a free-standing tape-recorder in an ordinary classroom. It is doubtful whether the aural feedback gives any significant advantage where the goal is communicative adequacy rather than near-native pronunciation.

More important, however, is the fact that installations with a central output permit only those rigidly controlled and tedious activities which have brought the laboratory into disrepute.

USING NEW TECHNOLOGY

Despite widespread and often enthusiastic discussion of Computer Assisted Language Learning (CALL) many members of the language-teaching profession remain sceptical of its value. Their doubts are of two kinds. Firstly, it is feared that the glamour of the computer may lead to its being used for tasks that could be more simply and more effectively achieved by other means. Secondly, and of greater moment, is the possibility that the demands of the computer may actually lead to a return to teaching methods inconsistent with our current understanding of the nature of language and the most appropriate ways of teaching it.

The constricting and rather mechanical nature of a device which must be preprogrammed appears to run counter to modern thinking which regards language as a flexible interpersonal skill involving real rather than simulated communication. From this point of view the computer may seem to share many of the supposed disadvantages of the language laboratory when it first came into use. Computer-simulated speech is entirely inauthentic and a long way indeed from resembling the responses of a natural, thinking human being.

The computer, indeed, seems better adapted to use of the written rather than the spoken medium and is, in that regard, even more favourable to traditional approaches than the old-fashioned laboratory. A number of often described and widely used programmes appear trivial beyond belief. Most language teachers, furthermore, do not have computer skills and are reluctant to become involved with computer technology until access to such skills is provided, either through substantial in-service courses or as a standard part of initial training.

These technophobic responses, however, come mainly from those without experience in the field, and there are arguments of a general kind for encouraging developments in the use of information technology in language teaching.

Computers have a strong motivational appeal for most pupils. Possibly the interest is a passing craze which will be as transient as hula hoops or Rubik's cube, and the time will come when the computer is as much taken for granted as the blackboard or even detested as the tape recorder was said to be by pupils using the Nuffield language courses. To date, however, there is little indication of this and the practice of obtaining information of all kinds from the computer is increasingly coming to be seen as part of everyday life.

Language teachers in the past have often suffered from the so-called sore thumb syndrome, being the one department in the school not able to accommodate new educational developments such as mixed-ability teaching, pupil-centred learning and block timetabling. It would be unfortunate if we were yet again to find ourselves out on a limb. Arguably, too, computer literacy is one of those general educational skills (GCSE Aim 7) to which modern languages, like all other subjects in the curriculum, should contribute.

It would also be surprising if there were not at least some aspects of the teaching of our subject that would benefit from the use of the computer. In our endeavour to maximise the effectiveness of our teaching we are therefore bound, however critically, to encourage research and experimentation in this field. This is necessary at two levels.

Firstly and obviously there is a need to encourage formal research and development projects and publishing ventures. No doubt, many such ventures will be misguided and prove abortive. Such is the price of evolutionary progress.

Equally important is experimentation at school level by departments and individual teachers. In the end, only actual users are able to judge the usefulness of this or that programme in comparison with others, or with entirely different methodologies. Such experimentation needs to be undertaken with both open-mindedness and caution, constantly monitoring innovation in terms of output. Ultimately, the only relevant question is 'Does it deliver the goods?' or 'Is it likely to do so in the end?' What is new is not necessarily meretricious, but novelty alone is no criterion of value.

In reply to some of the particular anxieties of language teachers mentioned above, it is well to begin by pointing out that the computer bears only the most superficial resemblance to the language laboratory. An essential feature of the language laboratory, at least in its traditional form, was that the pupil spends much time fairly passively listening and repeating, or at most making minimal changes of an analogical kind. With the computer, even at its most limited and unimaginative, the pupil is actively involved in typing in responses from a range of options of one kind or another.

As was suggested earlier, furthermore, the laboratory itself has not entirely outlived its usefulness or even fully realised its potential, and will no doubt eventually profit from the incorporation of computer-control technology, disc storage and so on.

The question of synthesised speech and speech recognition are something of a red herring. At the risk of joining in the hall of fame who predicted that *Le Cid* would not be remembered beyond the season of its first performance, or that the internal combustion engine could not be expected to replace the horse, I think it unlikely that either facility has much contribution to make to language teaching in the foreseeable future. If computers are to talk they must do so by controlling prerecorded tape, or some similar medium. At present, it is to the eye rather than the ear that they make their most obvious appeal.

If gap-filling exercises and rote learning have any value, and there are obviously some computer-minded language teachers who think they have (Blamire 1987; Beaton *et al.* 1986: 39–45) it has to be said that the computer handles these things with great efficiency. Many third- and fourth-formers have devised their own programmes for these tasks and there is some danger that such programmes will proliferate.

Happily, however, computer-assisted language learning also appears to be developing along much more imaginative lines. The most successful approaches are based not on the models of grammar grind or audio-lingual mim–mem, but on the appealing development of adventure games. The player is presented with certain choices selected by keyboard or cursor. Sometimes a word or simple phrase or sentence may have to be typed in. Progress is scored until the supposed goal is reached, or the game brought to a close by sudden death.

In *Granville* (Jones *et al* 1986) the pupil is supposedly spending a holiday in the resort of that name. He is offered choices of entertainments, transport, menus of drinks and snacks and so on, all costed. The choices made may be wise or rash. The game finishes after five 'days', or when the pupil's 'money' runs out.

Neither sound nor video are used. The media employed are text and graphics – plus a printed town guide, with photographs.

A further promising development involves the use of video disc and a link with an audio tape recorder. In an experimental package created by the Shropshire Local Education Authority the pupil both hears and sees authentic French speakers in the authentic French setting of Dieppe. He is given certain shopping tasks, may choose whether or not to ask his way of a French policeman and sees the actual products he is to choose from. Graphics are used only as the pupil attempts to find his way to the appropriate shops by using the cursor.

There may be some temptation to see developments of this kind purely in terms of the interaction between the computer and the individual pupil. If we do this we shall be led to suppose that, for the most part, practice is being given in the receptive skills of listening or reading comprehension alone. We may then go on to complain that the ideal of providing one micro per pupil is a long way off, and see a situation in which several pupils are grouped around a single screen as a kind of inadequate compromise.

This, however, is to remain entrapped in the view of the computer as a kind of super-lab with each pupil working on a one-to-one basis with a single machine. It misses the point mentioned earlier that, particularly in a communicative approach to language teaching, the purpose of the aid is not to carry out the teaching task itself, but to provide something for pupils to talk about. In group work, using materials of the kind described above, one pupil may operate the controls, but the whole group will cooperate in deciding which choices to make, and will give him or her (one may need to make sure it is not always a him) instructions accordingly. It is found that, even without being told to do so, most groups quickly fall into the habit of giving, indeed often shouting, their instructions (*à gauche, des pommes, ins Kino*, etc.) in the foreign language. Active, communicative use of the language may therefore be encouraged, whether the activity is being done with a whole class, or in a smaller group as part of a circus of activities (Beaton *et al* 1986: 26–9).

In addition to the above radical and rather spectacular developments there are a number of other more mundane uses to which the computer may be put, and which may have some potential.

In multiple-choice comprehension, for example, a program may be used in conjunction with an audio recording or printed text (or short text on the screen). The pupil simply indicates his reply by pressing buttons rather than ticking boxes.

The advantage of this over multiple-choice work using conventional media is that the pupil may receive immediate feedback and different 'incorrect' responses may result in a variety of instructions, questions or clues (e.g. look up the word 'die Gift' in your dictionary. Ist Georg ein Mann oder ein Hund?', who does 'der Freund' refer to? etc.) before the pupil reads or listens to the original text or recording again and makes a further attempt.

A further highly feasible day-to-day use of the computer borrowed from English mother-tongue teachers involves using the word-processing facility as a way of developing pupils' writing and reading comprehension skills. Cloze exercises are an obvious possibility. These may vary from the simplest kind in which a few individual letters have been deleted from a familiar text to much more demanding ones in which a whole text, briefly glanced at, has to be reconstituted. Scrambled sentences or texts may be reordered and first drafts of many other writing tasks may be revised and printed out in their finalised form without endless crossing out and recopying. The word-processing facility may also be used for creating worksheet masters which may then be photocopied in bulk.

The problems of language teachers' relative lack of programming skills is to some extent alleviated by the existence of so-called authoring packages which enable teachers to produce some of their own materials without actually needing to be able to program themselves. Such packages are necessarily constricting. They enable teachers to use their own content, but only in the making of particular predetermined kinds of exercise. This may, however, be a reasonable compromise, leaving the computer experts to devise increasingly flexible authoring packages and teachers free to find or devise increasingly stimulating raw materials.

Teachers who are enthusiastic both about their own teaching and about computers will not be deterred from devoting a considerable amount of time and ingenuity to devising their own programs. In terms of the effective use of preparation time as opposed to personal experimentation, however, it may be more profitable to seek to become thoroughly familiar with what is, or is about to appear, on the market.

Computers are but one aspect of information technology that has language-teaching potential. Satellite TV, access to European Computer Information Services equivalent to our Oracle or Ceefax, and electronic mail-box facilities on an international scale have all been suggested as possible sources of up-to-date authentic materials and modes of authentic communication (Beaton *et al* 1986: 33–8). The existence of these exciting possibilities naturally raises the question of 'How far should we go down this road?' In terms of research and experimentation the answer is no doubt 'All the way'. Language is about communication and by the time our pupils reach middle life it may well be at least as natural to communicate by screen and keyboard as it is for us to use the telephone or pen and ink. There is therefore nothing 'artificial' or inauthentic about working with the computer in a foreign language. Though we may wish to see experimentation in the use of information technology for the purposes of language teaching pushed to the extreme limits, however, the question for the classroom teacher remains not 'What is the most spectacularly up-to-date technology available?' but 'What, in terms of our pupils learning, is the most profitable way to occupy this class during the short time available, given their limitations and mine?'

In this situation it is always tempting to continue with well-tried procedures which have hitherto proved satisfactory. One hesitates to advance too quickly for fear of compromising pupils' progress. Fortunately, however, with introducing the use of aids and technology into one's teaching one is not quite in the either/or dilemma modern language teachers have sometimes faced in the past when whole new methodologies were being advocated. At the present time there are no doubt some computer programs that would improve the effectiveness of any given five-year course, and to that extent the courses in question are less than maximally effective. If the department does not take the plunge it will fall further behind, year by year. The answer, however, is to go not for a holistic revolution ('From September all our language teaching will be computerised') but to experiment with the use of such few computer programs as do seem promising, increasing this cautiously as seems justified by results and the response of pupils. In that way one remains in touch with developments and gradually builds up the skill and interest within the department. One is thus in a position to use and recognise new materials as they become available and judge, on a basis of real experience, the exaggerated claims of those bandwagoneers who may try to tell us that theirs is the only way for our subject to be taught.

REVIEW AND ENHANCEMENT

1. With the aid of your lesson book, review in detail your work with one class during the last two to three weeks.
   (a) Consider whether any of the activities used would have been substantially enhanced by the use of visual aids, whether self-produced, projected or photocopied. Detail the extra time and trouble this would have involved and whether use of the aid in question would have been desirable, all things considered.

(b) Consider occasions on which you did use visual or other aids. Identify the objectives of the activities involved and assess the contribution of the aid used. Include the value of novelty and variety in your assessment.

(c) Consider various pieces of material used during the period under review. Assess whether it would have been better to use an alternative medium (i) in an ideal world, (ii) given the constraints of your particular teaching situation.

(d) Plan a detailed scheme of work with the same class for the next two to three weeks. For the purposes of professional development use as wide a variety of aids and equipment as possible, with the proviso that this does not actually hinder pupils' progress. Log extra time and effort involved and note any improvement in class response and performance.

2. Analyse arrangements for the management and storage of aids and materials in your department.

(a) Over a period of two to three weeks log occasions on which inconvenience or uncertain availability have prevented you from using aids or equipment. Consider any feasible arrangements that would have prevented such incidents.

(b) Note any drawbacks or additional adminstrative burden of such arrangements. Discuss your conclusions with colleagues with a view to identifying support for changes of practice.

(c) Review your use of the language laboratory (if available). Consider whether this can, with advantage, be extended or adapted to meet current objectives.

(d) Review departmental equipment for producing aids and recordings. Identify any deficiencies that could be remedied at reasonable cost and press for this to be done.

3. If not already using CALL develop a personal policy for acquiring familiarity with information technology hardware and language-teaching software.

(a) Familiarise yourself with any other micro- or other computer used in the school and with software used in other subjects. Consider the feasibility of analogous materials for language teaching.

(b) Investigate the possibility of attending CALL courses offered nationally or locally.

(c) Investigate publishers' advertisements and descriptions of CALL software. Periodically request inspection materials or demonstrations from representatives. Arrange to visit colleagues known to be using CALL locally.

(d) Attempt to incorporate a limited but regular amount of CALL, however unadventurous, into your work for trial purposes. Increase as appropriate.

(e) If already using CALL extensively, examine your practice critically for its effectiveness in terms of your pupils' language achievement. Maintain and develop computer work where this has a clear advantage over other activities. Reassess the value of such activities as intensive and extensive listening and reading, oral class and group work and authentic writing tasks.

FURTHER READING

Ahmad K *et al* 1985 *Computers, Language Learning and Language Teaching*. Cambridge University Press, Cambridge

Beaton R *et al* 1986 *CALL for the Computer*. Loughborough, British Association for Language Teaching/Modern Language Association, Loughborough

Davies G and 1985 Higgins J *Using Computers in Language Learning*. Centre for Information on Language Teaching and Research, London

Smalley A and Morris D 1985 *The Modern Language Teacher's Handbook*. Hutchinson, London, pp 93–133, 213–223

BIBLIOGRAPHY

Abbott G and Wingard P 1981 *The Teaching of English as an International Language*. Collins, London

AEB 1985 *Specimen Materials: French. AEB, Guildford*

AEB 1986 *Revised Syllabus in Modern Languages for the First Examinations in 1988*. AEB, Guildford

Ahmad K *et al* 1985 *Computers Language Learning and Language Teaching*. Cambridge University Press, Cambridge

Beaton R *et al* 1986 *CALL for the Computer*. British Association for Language Teaching/Modern Language Association, London

Beattie N 1987 'Homework in the teaching and learning of modern languages 11–16', *British Journal of Language Teaching*, **25** (2) 67–72

Bird E 1981 'Sixth form language work', in Smith 1981a: 103–14

Blamire R 1987 'Using the computer for language learning, *Modern Languages* **68** (2) 122–27

Broughton, G. *et al* 1978 *Teaching English as a Foreign Language*. Routledge & Kegan Paul, London

Bruner J 1972 *The Relevance of Education*. George Allen & Unwin, London

Buckby M 1980–85 *Action! Graded French*. Nelson, Walton-on-Thames

Buckby M *et al* 1986 *Teaching Modern Languages for the GCSE*. British Association for Language Teaching/Modern Language Association, Leeds

Buckby M 1986 'Developing speaking skills in the GCSE in Buckby *et al*. 1986: 39–65

Chomsky N 1965 *Aspects of the Theory of Syntax*. MIT Press, Cambridge, Mass

Cohen B 1982 *Means and Ends in Education*. Allen & Unwin, London

Corless F 1978 'A new look at literary studies in the sixth form modern language course', *Audio-Visual Language Journal* **16** (3), 161–70

Council of Europe 1987 *Erasmus Newsletter*, 2/87, Council of Europe, Brussels

Davies G and Higgins J 1985 *Using Computers in Language Learning*. Centre for Information on Language Teaching and Research, London

Davies I K 1976 *Objectives in Curriculum Design*. McGraw-Hill, Maidenhead

DES 1984 *English 5–16. HMSO, London*

DES 1985 *General Certificate of Secondary Education; The National Criteria; French*. DES, London

DES 1987a *Modern Foreign Languages to 16*. HMSO, London

DES 1987b *The National Curriculum 5–16, A Consultation Document*. DES, London

Donmall B G (Ed.) 1985 *Language Awareness*. London Centre for Language Teaching and Research

Drucker P 1967 *The Effective Executive*. Pan, London

Emmans K Hawkins E and Westoby A 1974 *The Use of Foreign Languages in the Private Sector of Industry and Commerce*. York University Language Teaching Centre, York

Freudenstein R and James C V (Eds.) 1986 Confidence through Competence in Modern London, Centre for Information and Language Teaching and Research

Gilogley A C 1987 *Standard French*. Blackie, London

Girard D 1986 'Lecturing to Communicate in a foreign language' in Freudenstein and James (Eds.) 40–57

Godfrey I L 1987 'Setting up a TVEI French course at sixth form level', *British Journal of Language Teaching*, **25** (1) 3–7

Harris V and Roselman L 1986 *Tu Parles*! Arnold-Wheaton, Leeds

Hawkins E 1984 *Awarenes of Language: An Introduction* Cambridge University Press

HMI 1977 *Modern Languages in Comprehensive School*. HMSO, London PP 13–16

Hymes D 1972 'On communicative competence' in Pride and Holmes 1972: 269–93

JMB 1984 'Proposals for revision of the Advanced Level Modern Foreign Language, Syllabuses'. (typewritten consultative document). JMB, Manchester

JMB 1986 'Report on proposals for revision of the Advanced Level Modern Foreign Languages Syllabuses'. (typewritten document). JMB, Manchester Joint Matriculation Board

Jones B *et al* 1986 *Granville*. Cambridge University Press, Cambridge

Jupp T C and Hodlin S 1975 *Industrial English*. Heinemann Educational Books, London

Kelly A V 1975 *Case Studies in Mixed Ability Teaching*. Harper & Row, London

Littlewood W 1981 *Communicative Language Teaching*. Cambridge University Press, Cambridge

McNair J 1973 'Putting the question', *Modern Languages*. **54** (1), 27–31

Morgan G 1987 'Exploiting the natives – making use of native speakers in the classroom', *British Journal of Language Teaching*, **25** (2) 73–8

Munby J 1978 *Communicative Syllabus Design*. Cambridge University Press, Cambridge

NEA 1986 *French Syllabus for the 1989 Examination*. NEA, Manchester

NEA 1987 *French Syllabus for the 1989 Examination*. NEA, Manchester

Nicholls G C 1984 'The concept of communicative competence.' Unpublished M A thesis, University of Keele

Page B 1986 'Teaching listening skills for GCSE', in Buckby *et al.* 1986: 3–19

Partington J and Luker P 1984 *Teaching Modern Languages.* Macmillan, London

Pattison P 1987 *Developing Communication Skills.* Cambridge University Press, Cambridge

Peck A and Jury E 1987 *Orienteering: Listening Activities for GCSE German.* Mary Glasgow Publications, London

Perrott E 1982 *Effective Teaching.* Longman, London

Pride J B and Holmes J (eds) 1972 *Sociolinguistics.* Penguin, Harmondsworth

Robins J A 1986 'Hear! Hear! – an extension of listening comprehension' *British Journal of Language Teaching*, **24** (2) 93–7

Schools Council 1970 *Working Paper No. 28: New Patterns in Sixth Form Modern Language Studies.* Evans/Methuen, London

SCUE/CNAA 1986 *Standing Conference on University Entrance/council for National Academic Awards Guidelines for Written French at A Level.* SCUE/CNAA, London

Scullard S 1986 *Abgemacht.* Arnold Wheaton Leeds

SEC 1986 *French, GCSE, A Guide for Teachers.* Open University Press, Milton Keynes

Sidwell D and Capoore P 1984/5 *Deutsch Heute.* Nelson, Walton-on-Thames.

Slaney N 1986 'Conversations libres: beyond the conversation card', *British Journal of Language Teaching*, **24** (2) 98–103

Smalley A and Morris D 1985 *The Modern Language Teacher's Handbook.* Hutchinson, London

Smith D G (ed.) 1981a *Teaching Languages in Today's Schools.* Centre for Language Teaching and Research, London

Smith D G 1981b 'Sixth form 'A' level literature', in Simth 1981a: 115–26

Ur P 1984 *Teaching Listening Comprehension.* Oxford University Press, London

Van Ek J A 1976 *The Threshold Level.* Council of Europe, Strasburg

Walmsley R C 1975 'French', in Kelly 1975: 190–201

White J P 1973 *Towards a Compulsory Curriculum.* Routledge & Kegan Paul, London

Woods S 1986 Developing writing skills in the context of GCSE', in Buckby *et al*: 1986: 20–8

Wringe C A 1976 *Developments in Modern, Language Teaching.* Open Books, London

Wringe C A 1977 'The use of interaction analysis and microteaching in the training of modern language teachers, *NALA Journal*, **8** 40–4

Wringe C A 1988 *Understanding Educational Aims.* Unwin Hyman, London

INDEX

Abbott, G., 8, 49, 50, 52, 74
ability, teaching the full range of,
    112–17
acceptability, standards of, 6–7
Action! Graded French, 88–93
activities, timing and order of,
    32–6
Advanced Level, 12, 65, 120–32,
    see also sixth form teaching
Advanced Supplementary (A/S)
    Level, 72, 120
aims, 1–23
    in GCSE National Criteria, 1–2
    in *Modern Foreign Languages
    to 16*, 2
    non-linguistic, 11–21, 23
Alternative Ordinary (AO)
    Level, 120
assessment, 37–9
Associated Examining Board
    (AEB), 120, 130
attitudes
    positive towards foreign
    languages, 19–20
    required for further study,
    work and leisure, 11–13
authenticity, 5–6, 43–5

background reading, *see* sixth
    form teaching
Beaton, R., 147, 148
Beattie, N., 37
Blamire, R., 148
Broughton, G., 74
Bruner, J., 20
Buckby, M., 20, 66, 88

Capoore, P., 75
Certificate of Extended Education
    (CEE), 120
Certificate of Secondary
    Education (CSE), 113

Cohen, B., 87
communicative language teaching,
    1–11, 22
    as a slogan, 2
    contrasted with non-
    communicative approaches, 3
communicative syllabuses, 3–5
Computer Assisted Language
    Learning (CALL), 144–7,
    150–1, *see also* teaching aids
Council for National Academic
    Awards (CNAA), 121
Council of Europe, 12
culture and civilisation, 13–15,
    see also sixth form teaching

Daily Mirror, 93
degree courses, 121
Department of Education and
    Science (DES), 2, 11, 15, 19,
    74
Deutsch Heute, 75
differentiation,
    by ability, 112–17, 118
    by age, 104, 111
    importance of 104
Donmall, B.G., 15
Drucker, P., 1

Educational technology, *see*
    teaching aids
Emmans, K., 12
English as a Foreign Language,
    74
English 5–16, 15
enjoyment and stimulation, 17–19
essay writing, *see* sixth form
    teaching
European Economic Community
    (EEC), 13
European Studies, 14

examinations,
  see Advanced Level, Advanced
    Supplementary Level,
    General Certificate of
    Secondary Education, etc
  teaching in the examination
    year, *see* teaching methods
examining boards, *see* Associated
    Examining Board, Joint
    Matriculation Board,
    Northern Examining
    Association, etc.

functional syllabuses, 4–5
Further Education (FE), 120

General Certificate of Education
  (GCE), 113
General Certificate of Secondary
  Education (GCSE), 1–23,
  72–4, 120, 145
Gilogley, A. C., 75
Girard, D., 48–9
Godfrey, I. L., 120
Granville, 148
group work, *see* oral work in
  pairs and groups

Harris, V., 66
Hawkins, E. W., 12, 15
Her Majesty's Inspectors (HMI),
  1, 2, 113
Hodlin, S., 5
homework, 37
Hymes, D., 56

information gap activities, 9, 67–8
information technology, *see*
  Computer Assisted Language
  Learning
information transfer, 8

Joint Matriculation Board (JMB),
  12, 121, 130, 131
Jones, B., 146
Jury, E., 17
Jupp, T. C., 5

language/languages
  as a secondary skill, 13
  for further study, work and
    leisure, 11–13

insights into the nature of,
  15–17
introducing new language, 57–62,
  69–70
Language Awareness, 15–17
language functions, 4–5
language laboratory, 142–4, 150
listening and reading, 42–55
  modes of, 45–7, 54
literature, *see* sixth form teaching
Littlewood, W., 59
Luker, P., 74

McNair, J., 87
marking, 25, *see also* writing
materials and props, 31–2, *see*
  also teaching aids
  authenticity of, 43–5
medium, choice of, 137–8
memorisation, 137–8
Modern Foreign Languages to 16,
  2
Munby, J., 4

National Criteria for the GCSE
  in French, 1–23
Northern Examining Association
  (NEA), 4, 72, 80
News of the World, 93
Nicholls, G. C., 2
note-taking, 36–7

objectives, definition of, 22,
  29–31, 40–1
oral work in pairs and groups,
  62–70
  composition of groups, 69
  integration with other work,
    63–4
  open ended, 65–7
  varied complexity of, 64–5
  supervision and extension, 68–9
  see also speaking
overhead projector, 135–6, 7

Page, B., 7
pair work, *see* oral work in pairs
  and groups
Partington, J., 74
Pattison, P., 9
Peck, A., 17
Perrott, E., 4, 17, 87

planning
of individual lessons, 24–41
need for, 24–5
unit planning, 27–9
precommunicative activity, 9
presuppositions, indentification
of, 31
props, *see* materials and props

questioning, 87–103
on a fifth year text 87–93
on a second year text, 94–8
reasons for failure of, 102
value of, 87
questions
distribution of, 99–101
types of, 102
reading, see listening and
reading, sixth form work and
background reading
recording room, 141–2
recordings, teacher-made, 140–2
record keeping, 39–40, *see also*
note taking
redundancy, 49
Robins, J. A., 47
role-play, 67–8, 70, *see also* oral
working pairs and groups
Roselman, L., 66

scanning, *see* modes of listening
and reading
Secondary Examinations Council
(SEC), 2, 66
Scullard, S., 66
self-evaluation, 39–40
settings, 4
Sidwell, D., 75
sixth form teaching 120–33
background reading, 129–32
essay writing, 127–8
language work, 121–5
literature, 12, 121, 125–9
materials, 122
organisation of units, 123–5
target group, composition of
120–1
skills
four language skills, 7–8, 40
integration of, 6–7
learning skills of general
application, 20–1

receptive skills, *see* listening
and reading
skimming, *see* modes of listening
and reading
Slaney, N., 66
Smalley, A., 134
speaking 56–71
Standard French, 75
Standing Committee on
University Entrance (SCUE)
121
Sun, The 93
syllabuses
A-level, 12
communicative, 3–5

target language, use of, 9–11, 22,
128–9
tasks
authenticity of 43–5
language tasks, *see*
communicative syllabuses
presentation of language tasks,
56–7
teaching methods
appropriate to different
abilities, 112–7, 118
appropriate to different ages,
104–11, 117–18
communicative, 8–9
direct, 9–10
for beginners, 104–5
in the examination year, 110,
111, 118
in the middle years, 106–10,
117–18
in the 16–19 age range, 120–33
timing, 32–6, 41
teaching aids, 134–47
as a stimulus, 134–5
categories of, 134
economy in the use of, 135–7
management and storage,
135–40, 150
teacher made, 140–2, 150
testing, informal, 39–40, 41

Van Ek, J. A., 4, 5
video, 136

Walmsley, R. C., 115
Westoby, A., 12

White, J. P., 37
Wingard, P., 8, 49, 50, 52, 74
Woods, S., 74
worksheets, 136–7
writing, 72–86
  at basic and higher levels, 66
  correcting and marking, 79–86,
    see also acceptability,
    standards of

creating opportunities for,
  74–7
for communicative and
  pedagogic purposes, 73
writing activities, 77–9
writing test, pupils not taking,
  72–4
Wringe, C. A., 9, 28, 37, 87, 88,
  131